THE PRAYER LIFE

THE PRAYER LIFE

ANDREW MURRAY

moody press
chicago

ISBN: 0-8024-6806-3

Moody Press, a ministry of the Moody Bible Institute, is
designed for education, evangelization and edification.
If we may assist you in knowing more about Christ and
the Christian life, please write us without obligation to:
Moody Press, c/o MLM, Chicago, Illinois 60610.

CONTENTS

FOREWORD

A FEW WORDS with regard to the origin of this book and the object with which it was written will help to put the reader into the right position for understanding its teaching.

It was the outcome of a conference of ministers at Stellenbosch, South Africa, April 11-14, 1912. The occasion of the conference was as follows: Professor de Vos, of our Theological Seminary, had written a letter to the ministers of our church (Dutch Reformed Church) concerning the low state of spiritual life which marked the Church [Universal] generally, which [he said] ought to lead to the inquiry as to how far that statement included our church too. What had been said in the book, *The State of the Church,* called for deep searching of heart. He thought there could be no doubt about the truth of the statement in regard to the lack of spiritual power. He asked whether it was not time for us to come together and in God's presence to find out what might be the cause of the evil. He wrote: "If only we study the conditions in all sincerity, we shall have to acknowledge that our un-

7

belief and sin are the cause of the lack of spiritual power; that this condition is one of sin and guilt before God, and nothing less than a direct grieving of God's Holy Spirit."

His invitation met with a hearty response. Our four theological professors, with more than two hundred ministers, missionaries, and theological students, came together with the above words as the keynote of our meeting. From the very first in the addresses there was the tone of confession as the only way to repentance and restoration. At a subsequent meeting the opportunity was given for testimony as to what might be the sins which made the life of the Church so feeble. Some began to mention failings that they had seen in other ministers, either in conduct, or in doctrine, or in service. It was soon felt that this was not the right way; each must acknowledge that in which he himself was guilty.

The Lord graciously so ordered it that we were gradually led to the sin of prayerlessness as one of the deepest roots of the evil. No one could plead himself free from this. Nothing so reveals the defective spiritual life in minister and congregation as the lack of believing and unceasing prayer. Prayer is in very deed the pulse of the spiritual life. It is the great means of bringing to minister and people the blessing and power of heaven. Persevering and believing prayer means a strong and an abundant life.

When once the spirit of confession began to prevail, the question arose as to whether it would be indeed possible to expect to gain the victory over all that had in the past hindered our prayer life. In smaller conferences held previously, it had been found that many were most anxious to make a new beginning and yet had not the courage to expect that they would be able to maintain that prayer life which they saw to be in accordance with the Word of God. They had often made the attempt but had failed. They did not dare to make any promise to the Lord to live and pray as He would have them; they felt it impossible. Such confessions gradually led to the great truth, that the only power for a new prayer life is to be found in an entirely new relation to our blessed Saviour. It is as we see in Him the Lord who saves us from sin—the sin of prayerlessness too—and our faith yields itself to a life of closer intercourse with Him, that a life in His love and fellowship will make prayer to Him the natural expression of our soul's life. Before we parted, many were able to testify that they were returning with new light and new hope to find in Jesus Christ strength for a new prayer life.

Many felt that this was only a beginning. Satan, who had so long prevailed in the inner chamber, would do his utmost with his temptations to make us yield once again to the power of the flesh and the world. Nothing but the teaching and the fellowship of Christ Himself could ever give the power to remain faithful.

The need was felt for some statement of the truths that had been dealt with at the conference, to remind those who had been present of what they had learned and of what would help them in the new endeavor after that prayer life which is so essential to a minister's success. It was also needed for those who had been prevented from coming and for the eldership in our church, who had in many cases felt the deepest interest in hearing what the purpose was for which their ministers had gone from home.

Early copies of the book were sent out with the thought that if the leaders of the church, ministers and elders, begin to see that in spiritual work *everything depends upon prayer,* and that God Himself is the helper of those who wait on Him, it would indeed be a day of hope for our church. It was at the same time meant for all believers who long for a life of more entire separation to the Lord. For all who desired to pray more and pray better, it sought to point them to the glory of God in the inner chamber, and the way in which that glory can rest upon the soul.

When first asked to have the book translated into English, I felt as if its composition had been too hurried and its tone, owing to the close connection with the meetings that had preceded, too colloquial to make this desirable. And my own limited strength made it impossible for me to think of re-writing it. When, however, my friend, Rev. W. M. Douglas, asked permission to translate it, I gave my consent. If God has a message through the book to any of His servants, I would count it a privilege to tell what He has done here in our church, as a suggestion of what He may do in other churches.

I close with my greetings to all the ministers of the gospel and to the church members who may read these pages. I pray fervently that the grace of God that very manifestly wrought among us conviction of sin, confession of deep need and helplessness, and then gave the vision and the faith of what Jesus Christ can do for those who trust Him, may give to more than one who reads the courage to take counsel with his brethren and to seek for and obtain that full fellowship with God in prayer which is the very essence of the Christian life. It has been said: "It is only the prayerless who are too proud to own up to prayerlessness." Let us believe that there are many hearts waiting for the call inviting them to united and whole-hearted confession of shortcoming, as the only but the sure way of a return and restoration to God's favor, and the experience of what He will do in answer to prayer.

I wish to add one word more, in regard to "the Pentecostal prayer meetings" held throughout our church. These have had a very interesting and important place in our work. At the time of the great Revival in America and Ireland in 1858 and following years, some of our elder ministers issued a circular urging the churches to pray that God might visit us too. In 1860 the revival broke out in various parishes. In April, 1861, there was very deep interest shown in the Paarl, in one of our oldest congregations. During the week preceding Whitsunday, the minister, who ordinarily preached only once on a Sunday, announced that in the afternoon there would be a public prayer meeting in the church. The occasion was one of extraordinary interest, and many hearts were deeply touched. As one result the minister suggested that in the future the ten days between Ascension and Whitsunday should be observed by daily prayer meetings. This took place the following year. The blessing then received was such that all the neighboring congregations took up the suggestion, and now for fifty years the ten days of prayer have been observed throughout the whole church. Each year notes were issued as subjects of addresses and prayer, and the result has been that throughout our whole church Christians have been educated in the knowledge of what God's Word teaches regarding the Holy Spirit, and have been stirred to seek and to yield themselves to His blessed leading. These ten days have often proved the occasion for special effort with the unconverted, and of partial revival. And they have been the means of untold blessing in leading ministers and people to recognize the place that the Holy Spirit ought to have as the executive of the Godhead in the heart of the believer, in the dealing with souls, and in consecration to the service of the kingdom.

There is still very much indeed lacking of the full knowledge and power of the Holy Spirit, but we feel that we cannot be sufficiently grateful to God for what He has done through His leading us to dedicate these days to special prayer for the movings of His Holy Spirit.

I have written this with the thought that there may be some who will be glad to know of it, and in their sphere to unite in the observance.

ANDREW MURRAY

1

THE SIN AND CAUSE OF PRAYERLESSNESS

IF CONSCIENCE is to do its work, and the contrite heart is to feel its misery, it is necessary that each individual should mention his sin by name. The confession must be severely personal. In a meeting of ministers there is probably no single sin which each one of us ought to acknowledge with deeper shame—"Guilty, verily guilty"—than the sin of prayerlessness.

What is it, then, that makes prayerlessness such a great sin? At first it is looked upon merely as a weakness. There is so much talk about lack of time and all sorts of distractions that the deep guilt of the situation is not recognized. Let it be our honest desire that, for the future, the sin of prayerlessness may be to us truly sinful. Consider—

1. WHAT A REPROACH IT IS TO GOD.—There is the holy and most glorious God who invites us to come to Him, to hold converse with Him, to ask from Him such things as we need, and to experi-

ence what a blessing there is in fellowship with Him. He has created us in His own image, and has redeemed us by His own Son, so that in converse with Him we might find our highest glory and salvation.

What use do we make of this heavenly privilege? How many there are who take only five minutes for prayer! They say that they have no time and that the heart desire for prayer is lacking; they do not *know how* to spend half an hour with God! It is not that they absolutely do not pray; they pray every day—but they have no joy in prayer, as a token of communion with God which shows that God is every thing to them.

If a friend comes to visit them, they have time, they *make time,* even at the cost of sacrifice, for the sake of enjoying converse with him. Yes, they have time for everything that really interests them, but no time to practice fellowship with God and delight themselves in Him! They find time for a creature who can be of service to them; but day after day, month after month passes, and there is no time to spend *one hour* with God.

Do not our hearts begin to acknowledge what a dishonor, what a despite of God this is, that I dare to say I cannot find time for fellowship with Him? If this sin begins to appear plain to us, shall we not with deep shame cry out: "Woe is me, for I am undone, O God; be merciful to me, and forgive this awful sin of prayerlessness." Consider further—

2. IT IS THE CAUSE OF A DEFICIENT SPIRITUAL LIFE.—It is a proof that, for the most part, our life is still under the power of "the flesh." Prayer is the pulse of life; by it the doctor can tell what is the condition of the heart. The sin of prayerlessness is a proof for the ordinary Christian or minister that the life of God in the soul is in deadly sickness and weakness.

Much is said and many complaints are made about the feebleness of the Church to fulfill her calling, to exercise an influence over her members, to deliver them from the power of the world, and to bring them to a life of holy consecration to God. Much is also spoken about her indifference to the millions of heathen whom Christ entrusted to her that she might make known to them His love and salvation. What is the reason that many thousands of Christian workers in the world have not a greater influence? Nothing save this—the prayerlessness of their service. In the midst of all their zeal in the study and in the work of the Church, of all their faithfulness in preaching and conversation with the people, they lack that ceaseless prayer which has attached to it the sure promise of the Spirit and the power from on high. It is nothing but the sin of prayerlessness which is the cause of the lack of a powerful spiritual life! Consider further—

3. THE DREADFUL LOSS WHICH THE CHURCH SUFFERS AS A RESULT OF PRAYERLESSNESS OF THE MINISTER.——It is the business of a minister to train believers up to a life of prayer; but how can a leader do this if he himself understands little the art of conversing with God and of receiving from the Holy Spirit, every day, out of heaven, abundant grace for himself and for his work? A minister cannot lead a congregation higher than he is himself. He cannot with enthusiasm point out a way, or explain a work, in which he is not himself walking or living.

How many thousands of Christians there are who know next to nothing of the blessedness of prayer fellowship with God! How many there are who know something of it and long for a further increase of this knowledge, but in the preaching of the Word they are not persistently urged to keep on till they obtain the blessing! The reason is simply and only that the minister understands so little about the secret of powerful prayer and does not give prayer the place in his service which, in the nature of the case and in the will of God, is indispensably necessary. Oh, what a difference we should notice in our congregations if ministers could be brought to see in its right light the sin of prayerlessness and were delivered from it! Once more consider—

4. THE IMPOSSIBILITY OF PREACHING THE GOS-

PEL TO ALL MEN—as we are commanded by Christ to do—so long as this sin is not overcome and cast out.

Many feel that the great need of missions is the obtaining of men and women who will give themselves to the Lord to strive in prayer for the salvation of souls. It has also been said that God is eager and able to deliver and bless the world He has redeemed, if His people were but willing, if they were but ready, to cry to Him day and night. But how can congregations be brought to that unless there comes first an entire change in ministers and that they begin to see that the indispensable thing is not preaching, not pastoral visitation, not church work, but *fellowship with God in prayer till they are clothed with power from on high?*

Oh, that all thought and work and expectation concerning the kingdom might drive us to the acknowledgement of the sin of prayerlessness! God help us to root it out! God deliver us from it through the blood and power of Christ Jesus! God teach every minister of the Word to see what a glorious place he may occupy if he first of all is delivered from this root of evils; so that with courage and joy, in faith and perseverance, he can go on with his God!

The sin of prayerlessness! The Lord lay the burden of it so heavy on our hearts that we may not rest till it is taken far from us through the name and power of Jesus. He will make this possible for us.

A Witness from America

In 1898, there were two members of the Presbytery in New York who attended the Northfield Conference for the deepening of the spiritual life. They returned to their work with the fire of a new enthusiasm. They endeavored to bring about a revival in the entire Presbytery. In a meeting which they held, the chairman was guided to ask the brethren a question concerning their prayer life: "Brethren," said he, "let us today make confession before God and each other. It will do us good. Will everyone who spends half an hour every day with God in connection with his work hold up a hand?" One hand was held up. He made a further request: "All who thus spend fifteen minutes hold up a hand." Not half of the hands were held up. Then he said: "Prayer, the working power of the Church of Christ, and half of the workers make hardly any use of it! All who spend five minutes hold up hands." All hands went up. But one man came later with the confession that he was not quite sure if he spent five minutes in prayer every day. "It is," said he, "a terrible revelation of how little time I spend with God."

The Cause of Prayerlessness

In an elder's prayer meeting, a brother put the question: "What, then, is the cause of so much prayerlessness? Is it not unbelief?"

The answer was: "Certainly; but then comes the question—what is the cause of that unbelief?" When the disciples asked the Lord Jesus: "Why could not we cast the devil out?" His answer was: "Because of your unbelief." He went further and said: "Howbeit this kind goeth not out but by prayer and fasting." If the life is not one of self-denial—of fasting—that is, letting the world go; of prayer—that is, laying hold of heaven, faith cannot be exercised. A life lived according to the flesh and not according to the Spirit—it is in this that we find the origin of the prayerlessness of which we complain. As we came out of the meeting, a brother said to me: "That is the whole difficulty; we wish to pray in the Spirit and at the same time walk after the flesh, and this is impossible."

If one is sick and desires healing, it is of prime importance that the true cause of the sickness be discovered. This is always the first step toward recovery. If the particular cause is not recognized, and attention is directed to subordinate causes, or to supposed but not real causes, healing is out of the question. In like manner, it is of the utmost importance for us to obtain a correct insight into the cause of the sad condition of deadness and failure in prayer in the inner chamber, which should be such a blessed place for us. Let us seek to realize fully what is the root of this evil.

Scripture teaches us that there are but two conditions possible for the Christian. One is a walk according to the Spirit, the other a walk according to "the flesh." These two powers are in irreconcilable conflict with each other. So it comes to pass, in the case of the majority of Christians, that, while we thank God that they are born again through the Spirit and have received the life of God—yet their ordinary daily life is not lived according to the Spirit but according to "the flesh." Paul writes to the Galatians: "Are ye so foolish? having begun in the Spirit, are ye now made perfect by the flesh?" (Gal. 3:3). Their service lay in fleshly outward performances. They did not understand that where "the flesh" is permitted to influence their service of God, it soon results in open sin.

So he mentions not only grave sins as the work of "the flesh," such as adultery, murder, drunkenness; but also the more ordinary sins of daily life—wrath, strife, variance; and he gives the exhortation: "Walk in the Spirit, and ye shall not fulfill the lust of the flesh. . . . If we live in the Spirit, let us also walk in the Spirit" (Gal. 5:16, 25). The Spirit must be honored not only as the Author of a new life but also as the Leader and Director of our entire walk. Otherwise we are what the apostle calls "carnal."

The majority of Christians have little understanding of this matter. They have no real knowledge of the deep sinfulness and godlessness of that carnal nature which belongs to them and to which unconsciously they yield. "God . . . condemned sin in the flesh" (Rom. 8:3)—in the cross of Christ. "They that are Christ's have crucified the flesh with the affections and lusts" (Gal. 5:24). "The flesh" cannot be improved or sanctified. "The carnal mind is *enmity against God; for it is not subject to the law of God, neither indeed can be*" (Rom. 8:7). There is no means of dealing with "the flesh" save as Christ dealt with it, bearing it to the cross. "Our old man is crucified with him" (Rom. 6:6); so we by faith also crucify it, and regard and treat it daily as an accursed thing that finds its rightful place on the accursed cross.

It is saddening to consider how many Christians there are who seldom think or speak earnestly about the deep and immeasurable sinfulness of "the flesh"—"In me (that is, in my flesh) dwelleth no good thing" (Rom. 7:18). The man who truly believes this may well cry out: "I see another law in my members . . . bringing me into captivity to the law of sin . . . O wretched man that I am! Who shall deliver me from the body of this death?" (Rom. 7:23, 24). Happy is he who can go further and

23

say: "I thank God, through Jesus Christ our Lord. . . . *For the law of the Spirit of life in Christ Jesus hath made me free* from the law of sin and death" (Rom. 7:25; 8:2).

Would that we might understand God's counsels of grace for us! "The flesh" on the cross—the Spirit in the heart and controlling the life.

This spiritual life is too little understood or sought after; yet it is literally what God has promised and will accomplish in those who unconditionally surrender themselves to Him for this purpose.

Here then we have the deep root of evil as the cause of a prayerless life. "The flesh" can say prayers well enough, calling itself religious for so doing and thus satisfying conscience. But "the flesh" has no desire or strength for the prayer that strives after an intimate knowledge of God; that rejoices in fellowship with Him; and that continues to lay hold of His strength. So, finally, it comes to this, "the flesh" must be denied and crucified.

The Christian who is still carnal has neither disposition nor strength to follow after God. He rests satisfied with the prayer of habit or custom; but the glory, the blessedness of secret prayer is a hidden thing to him, till some day his eyes are opened, and he begins to see that "the flesh," in its disposition to turn away from God, is the archenemy which makes powerful prayer impossible for him.

I had once, at a conference, spoken on the subject of prayer and made use of strong expressions about the enmity of "the flesh" as a cause of prayer-lessness. After the address, the minister's wife said that she thought I had spoken too strongly. She also had to mourn over too little desire for prayer, but she knew her heart was sincerely set on seeking God. I showed her what the Word of God said about "the flesh," and that everything which prevents the reception of the Spirit is nothing else than a secret work of "the flesh." Adam was created to have fellowship with God and enjoyed it before his Fall. After the Fall, however, there came immediately, a deep-seated aversion to God, and he fled from Him. This incurable aversion is the characteristic of the unregenerate nature and the chief cause of our unwillingness to surrender ourselves to fellowship with God in prayer. The following day she told me that God had opened her eyes; she confessed that the enmity and unwillingness of "the flesh" was the hidden hindrance in her defective prayer life.

O my brethren, do not seek to find in circumstances the explanation of this prayerlessness over which we mourn; seek it where God's Word declares it to be, in the hidden aversion of the heart to a holy God.

When a Christian does not yield entirely to the leading of the Spirit—and this is certainly the will of God and the work of His grace—he lives, without knowing it, under the power of "the flesh." This life of "the flesh" manifests itself in many different ways. It appears in the hastiness of spirit, or the anger which so unexpectedly arises in you, in the lack of love for which you have so often blamed yourself; in the pleasure found in eating and drinking, about which at times your conscience has chidden you; in that seeking for your own will and honor, that confidence in your own wisdom and power, that pleasure in the world, of which you are sometimes ashamed before God. All this is life "after the flesh." "Ye are yet carnal" (I Cor. 3:3)—that text, perhaps, disturbs you at times; you have not full peace and joy in God.

I pray you take time and give an answer to the question: Have I not found here the cause of my prayerlessness, of my powerlessness to effect any change in the matter? I live in the Spirit, I have been born again, but I do not walk after the Spirit— "the flesh" lords it over me. The carnal life cannot possibly pray in the spirit and power. God forgive me. The carnal life is evidently the cause of my sad and shameful prayerlessness.

The Storm Center on the Battlefield

Mention was made in conference of the expression "strategic position" used so often in reference to the great strife between the kingdom of heaven and the powers of darkness.

When a general chooses the place from which he intends to strike the enemy, he pays most attention to those points which he thinks most important in the fight. Thus there was on the battlefield of Waterloo a farmhouse which Wellington immediately saw was the key to the situation. He did not spare his troops in his endeavor to hold that point: the victory depended on it. So it actually happened. It is the same in the conflict between the believer and the powers of darkness. The inner chamber is the place where the decisive victory is obtained.

The enemy uses all his power to lead the Christian, and above all the minister, to neglect prayer. He knows that however admirable the sermon may be, however attractive the service, however faithful the pastoral visitation, none of these things can damage him or his kingdom if prayer is neglected. When the Church shuts herself up to the power of the inner chamber, and the soldiers of the Lord have received on their knees "power from on high," then the powers of darkness will be shaken and souls will be delivered. In the Church, on the mission field, with the minister and his congregation, everything depends on the faithful exercise of the power of prayer.

In the week of conference I found the following in *The Christian:*

Two persons quarrel over a certain point. We call them Christian and Apollyon. Apollyon notices that

Christian has a certain weapon which would give him a sure victory. They meet in deadly strife, and Apollyon resolves to take away the weapon from his opponent and destroy it. For the moment the main cause of the strife has become subordinate; the great point now is who shall get possession of the weapon on which everything depends? It is of vital importance to get hold of that.

So it is in the conflict between Satan and the believer. God's child can conquer everything by prayer. Is it any wonder that Satan does his utmost to snatch that weapon from the Christian, or to hinder him in the use of it?

How now does Satan hinder prayer? By temptation to postpone or curtail it, by bringing in wandering thoughts and all sorts of distractions; through unbelief and hopelessness. Happy is the prayer hero who, through it all, takes care to hold fast and use his weapon. Like our Lord in Gethsemane, the more violently the enemy attacked the more earnestly He prayed and ceased not till He had obtained the victory. After all the other parts of the armor had been named, Paul adds: "With all prayer and supplication in the Spirit" (Eph. 6:18). Without prayer, the helmet of salvation, and the shield of faith, and the Sword of the Spirit, which is God's Word, have no power. All depends on prayer. God teach us to believe and hold this fast!

2

THE FIGHT AGAINST PRAYERLESSNESS

As soon as the Christian becomes convinced of his sin in this matter, his first thought is that he must begin to strive, with God's help, to gain the victory over it. But alas, he soon experiences that his striving is worth little, and the discouraging thought comes over him, like a wave, that such a life is not for him—he cannot continue faithful! At conferences on the subject of prayer, held during the past years, many a minister has openly said that it seemed impossible for him to attain such a strict life.

Recently I received a letter from a minister, well known for his ability and devotion, in which he writes: "As far as I am concerned, it does not seem to help me to hear too much about the life of prayer, about the strenuous exertion for which we must prepare ourselves, and about all the time and trouble and endless effort it will cost us. These things discourage me—I have so often heard them.

I have time after time put them to the test, and the result has always been sadly disappointing. It does not help me to be told: "You must pray more, and hold a closer watch over yourself, and become altogether a more earnest Christian."

My reply to him was as follows: "I think in all I spoke at the conference or elsewhere, I have never mentioned exertion or struggle, because I am so entirely convinced that our efforts are futile unless we first learn how to abide in Christ by a simple faith."

My correspondent said further: "The message I need is this: 'See that your relationship to your living Saviour is what it ought to be. Live in His presence, rejoice in His love, rest in Him.'" A better message could not be given, if it is only rightly understood. "See that your relationship to the living Saviour is what it ought to be." But this is just what will certainly make it possible for one to live the life of prayer.

We must not comfort ourselves with the thought of standing in a right relationship to the Lord Jesus while the sin of prayerlessness has power over us, and while we, along with the whole Church, have to complain about our feeble life which makes us unfit to pray for ourselves, for the Church, or for missions, as we ought. But if we recognize, in the first place, that a right relationship to the Lord Jesus, above all else, includes prayer, with both the desire and power to pray according to God's will, then we have something which gives us the right to rejoice in Him and to rest in Him.

I have related this incident to point out how naturally discouragement will be the result of self-effort and will so shut out all hope of improvement or victory. And this indeed is the condition of many Christians when called on to persevere in prayer as intercessors. They feel it is something entirely beyond their reach—they have not the power for the self-sacrifice and consecration necessary for such prayer; they shrink from the effort and struggle which will, as they suppose, make them unhappy. They have tried in the power of the flesh to conquer the flesh—a wholly impossible thing. They have endeavored by Beelzebub to cast out Beelzebub—and this can never happen. It is Jesus alone who can subdue the flesh and the devil.

We have spoken of a struggle which will certainly result in disappointment and discouragement. This is the effort made in our own strength. But there is another struggle which will certainly lead to victory. The Scripture speaks of "the good fight of faith," that is to say, a fight which springs from and is carried on by faith. We must get right conceptions about faith and stand fast in our faith. Jesus Christ is ever the Author and Finisher of faith. It is when we come into right relationship with Him that we can be sure of the help and power He bestows. Just, then, as earnestly as we must, in the first place, say: "Do not strive in your own strength; cast yourself at the feet of the Lord Jesus, and wait upon Him in the sure confidence that He is with you, and works in you"; so do we, in the second place, say: "Strive in prayer; let faith fill your heart—so will you be strong in the Lord, and in the power of His might."

An illustration will help us to understand this. A devoted Christian woman who conducted a large Bible class with zeal and success once came in trouble to her minister. In her earlier years she had enjoyed much blessing in the inner chamber, in fellowship with the Lord and His Word. But this had gradually been lost and, do what she would, she could not get right. The Lord had blessed her work, but the joy had gone out of her life. The minister asked what she had done to regain the lost blessedness. "I have done everything," said she, "that I can think of, but all in vain."

He then questioned her about her experience in connection with her conversion. She gave an immediate and clear answer: "At first I spared no pains in my attempt to become better, and to free myself from sin, but it was all useless. At last I began to understand that I must lay aside all my efforts, and simply trust the Lord Jesus to bestow on me His life and peace, and He did it."

"Why then," said the minister, "do you not try

this again? As you go to your inner chamber, however cold and dark your heart may be, do not try in your own might to force yourself into the right attitude. Bow before Him, and tell Him that He sees in what a sad state you are and that your only hope is in Him. Trust Him with a childlike trust to have mercy upon you, and wait upon Him. In such a trust you are in a right relationship to Him. You have nothing—He has everything." Some time later she told the minister that his advice had helped her; she had learned that faith in the love of the Lord Jesus is the only method of getting into fellowship with God in prayer.

Do you not begin to see, my reader, that there are two kinds of warfare—the first when we seek to conquer prayerlessness in our own strength. In that case, my advice to you is: "Give over your restlessness and effort; fall helpless at the feet of the Lord Jesus; He will speak the word, and your soul will live." If you have done this, then, second, comes the message: "This is but the beginning of everything. It will require deep earnestness, and the exercise of all your power, and a watchfulness of the entire heart—eager to detect the least backsliding. Above all, it will require a surrender to a life of self-sacrifice that God really desires to see in us and which He will work out for us."

3

HOW TO BE DELIVERED FROM PRAYERLESSNESS; HOW DELIVERANCE MAY CONTINUE

THE GREATEST STUMBLING-BLOCK in the way of victory over prayerlessness is the secret feeling that we shall never obtain the blessing of being delivered from it. Often have we put forth effort in this direction, but in vain. Old habit and the power of the flesh, our surroundings with their attractions, have been too strong for us. What good is it to attempt that which our heart assures us is out of our reach? The change needed in the entire life is too great and too difficult. If the question is put: "Is a change possible?" our sighing heart says: "Alas, for me it is entirely impossible!" Do you know why that reply comes? It is simply because you have received the call to prayer as the voice of Moses and as a command of the law. Moses and his law have never yet given anyone the power to obey.

Do you really long for the courage to believe that

deliverance from a prayerless life is possible for you and may become a reality? Then you must learn the great lesson that such a deliverance is included in the redemption that is in Christ Jesus, that it is *one of the blessings of the New Covenant which God Himself will impart to you through Christ Jesus.* As you begin to understand this you will find that the exhortation, "Pray without ceasing," conveys a new meaning. Hope begins to spring up in your heart that the Spirit—who has been bestowed on you to cry constantly, "Abba, Father"—will make a true life of prayer possible for you. Then you will hearken, not in the spirit of discouragement, but in the gladness of hope, to the voice that calls you to repentance.

Many a one has turned to his inner chamber, under bitter self-accusation that he has prayed so little, and has resolved for the future to live in a different manner. Yet no blessing has come—there was not the strength to continue faithful, and the call to repentance had no power, because his eyes had not been fixed on the Lord Jesus. If he had only understood, he would have said: "Lord, Thou seest how cold and dark my heart is: I know that I must pray, but I feel I cannot do so; I lack the urgency and desire to pray."

He did not know that at that moment the Lord Jesus in His tender love was looking down upon him and saying: "You cannot pray; you feel that all is cold and dark: why not give yourself over into My hands? Only believe that I am ready to help you in prayer; I long greatly to shed abroad My love in your heart, so that you, in the consciousness of weakness, may confidently rely on Me to bestow the grace of prayer. Just as I will cleanse you from all other sins, so also will I deliver from the sin of prayerlessness—only do not seek the victory in your own strength. Bow before Me as one who expects everything from his Saviour. Let your soul keep silence before Me, however sad you feel your state to be. Be assured of this—I will teach you how to pray."

Many a one will acknowledge: "I see my mistake; I had not thought that the Lord Jesus must deliver and cleanse me from this sin also. I had not understood that He was with me every day in the inner chamber, in His great love ready to keep and bless me, however sinful and guilty I felt myself to be. I had not supposed that just as He will give all other grace in answer to prayer, so, above all and before all, He will bestow the grace of a praying heart. What folly to think that all other blessings must come from Him, but that prayer, whereon everything else depends, must be obtained by personal effort! Thank God I begin to comprehend—the Lord Jesus is Himself in the inner chamber watching over me, and holding Himself responsible to teach me how to approach the Father.

This only He demands—that I, with childlike confidence, wait upon Him and glorify Him."

Brethren, have we not seriously forgotten this truth? From a defective spiritual life nothing better can be expected than a defective prayer life. It is vain for us, with our defective spiritual life, to endeavor to pray more or better. *It is an impossibility.* Nothing less is necessary than that we should experience that he who "is in Christ Jesus is a new creature: old things have passed away; behold, all things are become new." This is literally true for the man who understands and experiences what it is to be in Jesus Christ.

Our whole relationship to the Lord Jesus must be a new thing. I must believe in His infinite love, which really longs to have communion with me every moment and to keep me in the enjoyment of His fellowship. I must believe in His divine power, which has conquered sin and will truly keep me from it. I must believe in Him who, as the great Intercessor, through the Spirit, will inspire each member of His Body with joy and power for communion with God in prayer. My prayer life must be brought entirely under the control of Christ and His love. Then, for the first time, will prayer become what it really is, the natural and joyous breathing of the spiritual life, by which the heavenly atmosphere is inhaled and then exhaled in prayer.

Do you not see that, just as this faith possesses us, the call to a life of prayer which pleases God will be a welcome call? The cry, "Repent of the sin of prayerlessness," will not be responded to by a sigh of helplessness, or by the unwillingness of the flesh. The voice of the Father will be heard as He sets before us a widely opened door and receives us into blessed fellowship with Himself. Prayer for the help of the Spirit to pray will no longer be in fear of an effort too great for our power; it will be but falling down in utter weakness at the feet of the Lord Jesus, to find there that victory comes through the might and love which stream from His countenance.

If the question arises in our mind: Will this continue? and the fear comes: "You know how often you have tried and been disappointed," faith will find its strength, not in the thought of what you will, or do, but in the changeless faithfulness and love of Christ, who afresh has succored you and assured you that those who wait on Him shall not be ashamed.

If fear and hesitation still remain, I pray you by the mercies of God in Jesus Christ, and by the unspeakable faithfulness of His tender love, dare to cast yourselves at His feet. Only believe with your whole heart that there is deliverance from the sin of prayerlessness. "If we confess our sins, he is faithful and just to forgive us our sins, and to cleanse us from all unrighteousness" (I John 1:9). In His blood and grace there is complete deliverance from all unrighteousness and from all prayerlessness. Praised be His name forever!

How Deliverance from Prayerlessness May Continue

What we have said about deliverance from the sin of prayerlessness has also application as answer to the question: "How may the experience of deliverance be maintained?" Redemption is not granted to us piecemeal, or as something of which we may make use from time to time. It is bestowed as *a fullness of grace stored up in the Lord Jesus, which may be enjoyed in a new fellowship with Him every day.* It is so necessary that this great truth should be driven home and fastened in our minds that I will once more mention it. Nothing can preserve you from carelessness, or make it possible for you to preserve in living, powerful prayer, but a daily close fellowship with Jesus our Lord.

He said to His disciples: "Ye believe in God, *believe also in me. . . . Believe me* that I am in the Father, and the Father in me. . . . He that believeth on me, the works that I do shall he do also; and greater works than these shall he do" (John 14:1, 11, 12).

The Lord wished to teach His disciples that all they had learned from the Old Testament concerning the power and holiness and love of God must now be transferred to Him. They must not believe merely in certain written documents but in Him personally. They must believe that He was in the Father, and the Father in Him, in such a sense that they had *one* life, *one* glory. All that they knew about Christ they would find in God. He laid much emphasis on this because it was only through such a faith in Him and His divine glory that they could do the works which He did, or even greater works. This faith would lead them to know that just as Christ and the Father are One, so also they were in Christ and Christ was in them.

It is this intimate, spiritual, personal, uninterrupted relationship to the Lord Jesus which manifests itself powerfully in our lives, and especially in our prayer lives. Let us consider this and see what it means: that all the glorious attributes of God are in our Lord Jesus Christ. Think of—

1. GOD'S OMNIPRESENCE, with which He fills the world and every moment is present in everything. Just as it is with the Father, so now our Lord Jesus is everywhere present, above all with each of His redeemed ones. This is one of the greatest and most important lessons which our faith must learn. We can clearly understand this from the example of our Lord's disciples. What was the peculiar privilege of these disciples, who were always in fellowship with Him? It was *uninterrupted enjoy-*

ment of the presence of the Lord Jesus. It was because of this they were so sorrowful at the thought of His death. They would be deprived of that presence. He would be no longer with them. How, under these circumstances, did the Lord Jesus comfort them? He promised that the Holy Spirit from heaven should so work in them a sense of the fullness of His life and of His personal presence that He would be even more intimately near and have more unbroken fellowship with them than ever they experienced while He was upon earth.

This great promise is now the inheritance of every believer, although so many of them know little about it. Jesus Christ, in His divine personality, in that eternal love which led Him to the cross, longs to have fellowship with us every moment of the day and to keep us in the enjoyment of that fellowship. This ought to be explained to every new convert: "The Lord loves you so that He would have you near Him without a break, that you may have experience of His love." This is what every believer must learn who has felt his powerlessness for a life of prayer, of obedience, and of holiness. This alone will give us power as intercessors to conquer the world and to win souls out of it for our Lord.

2. THE OMNIPOTENCE OF GOD.—How wonderful is God's power! We see it in Creation; we see it in the wonders of redemption recorded in the Old

Testament. We see it in the wonderful works of Christ which the Father wrought in Him, and above all in His resurrection from the dead. We are called on to believe in the Son, just as we believe in the Father. Yes, the Lord Jesus who, in His love, is so unspeakably near us, is the Almighty One with whom nothing is impossible. Whatever may be in our hearts or flesh, which will not submit to us, He can and will conquer. Everything that is promised in God's Word, all that is our inheritance as children of the New Covenant, the Almighty Jesus can bestow upon us. *If I bow before Him in my inner chamber, then I am in contact with the eternal, unchanging power of God.* If I commit myself for the day to the Lord Jesus, then I may rest assured that it is His eternal almighty power which has taken me under its protection and which will accomplish everything for me.

Oh, if we would only take time for the inner chamber so that we might experience in full reality the presence of this Almighty Jesus! What a blessedness would be ours through faith! An unbroken fellowship with an Omnipotent and Almighty Lord.

3. THE HOLY LOVE OF GOD.—This means that He, with His whole heart, offers all His divine attributes for our service and is prepared to impart Himself to us. Christ is the revelation of His love. He is the Son of His love—the Gift of His love— the power of His love; and this Jesus, who has

sought on the cross to give an overwhelming proof of His love in His death and bloodshedding, so as to make it impossible for us not to believe in that love—this Jesus is He who comes to meet us in the inner chamber, and gives the positive assurance *that unbroken fellowship with Him is our inheritance, and will, through Him, become our experience.* The holy love of God which sacrificed everything to conquer sin and bring it to naught, comes to us in Christ to save us from every sin.

Brethren, take time to think over that word of our Lord: "Ye believe in God, believe also in me." "Believe me that I am in the Father, and ye in me, and I in you." That is the secret of the life of prayer. Take time in the inner chamber to bow down and worship; and wait on Him till he unveils Himself, and takes possession of you, and goes out with you to show how a man may live and walk in abiding fellowship with an unseen Lord.

Do you long to know how you may always experience deliverance from the sin of prayerlessness? Here you have the secret. Believe in the Son of God, give Him time in the inner chamber to reveal Himself in His ever present nearness, as the Eternal and Almighty One, the Eternal Love who watches over you. You will experience what, up till now, you have perhaps not known—that it has not entered into the heart of man what God can do for those who love Him.

4

THE BLESSING OF VICTORY; THE MORE ABUNDANT LIFE

IF NOW we are delivered from the sin of prayerlessness, and understand how this deliverance may continue to be experienced, what will be the fruit of our liberty? He who sees this aright will, with renewed earnestness and perseverance, seek after this liberty. His life and experience will indeed be an evidence that he has obtained something of unspeakable worth. He will be a living witness of the blessing which victory has brought. Consider—

1. THE BLESSEDNESS OF UNBROKEN FELLOWSHIP WITH GOD. Think of the confidence in the Father which will take the place of the reproach and self-condemnation which was the earlier characteristic of our lives. Think of the deep consciousness that God's almighty grace has effected something in us, to prove that we really bear His image and are fitted for a life of communion with Him and prepared to glorify Him. Think how we, notwith-

standing our conviction of our nothingness, may live as true children of a King, in communion with their Father, and may manifest something of the character of our Lord Jesus in the holy fellowship with His Father which He had when on earth. Think how in the inner chamber the hour of prayer may become the happiest time in the whole day for us, and how God may use us to take a share in the carrying out of His plans, and make us fountains of blessing for the world around us.

2. THE POWER WHICH WE MAY HAVE FOR THE WORK TO WHICH WE ARE CALLED. The preacher will learn to receive his message really from God, through the power of the Holy Spirit, and to deliver it in that power to the congregation. He will know where he can be filled with the love and zeal which will enable him, in his rounds of pastoral visiting, to meet and help each individual in a spirit of tender compassion. He will be able to say with Paul: "I can do all things through Christ who strengtheneth me." "We are more than conquerors through him that loved us." "We are ambassadors for Christ . . . we pray you in Christ's stead, be ye reconciled to God." These are no vain dreams or pictures of a foolish imagination. God has given us Paul as an illustration, so that, however we may differ from him in gifts or calling, yet in inner experience we may know the all-sufficiency of grace which can do all things for us as it did for him.

3 THE PROSPECT WHICH OPENS BEFORE US FOR THE FUTURE—*to be consecrated to take part as intercessors in the great work of bearing on our hearts the need of the entire Church and world.* Paul sought to arouse men to pray for all saints, and he tells us what a conflict he had for those who had not yet seen his face. In his personal presence he was subject to conditions of time and place, but in the Spirit he had power in the name of Christ to pray for blessing on those who had not yet heard of the Saviour. In addition to his life in connection with men here on earth, far or near, he lived another, a heavenly life—one of love and of a wonderful power in prayer which he continually exercised. We can hardly form a conception of the power God will bestow, if only we get freed from the sin of prayerlessness and pray with the daring which reaches heaven and brings down blessing in the almighty name of Christ.

What a prospect! Minister and missionaries brought by God's grace to pray, let us say twice as much as formerly, with twofold faith and joy! What a difference it would make in the preaching, in the prayer meeting, in the fellowship with others! *What a gentle power would come down in an inner chamber, sanctified by communion with God and His love in Christ!* What an influence would be exercised on believers, in urging them forward to the work of intercession! How greatly would this influence be felt in the Church and among the heathen! What power might be exercised over ministers of other churches, and who knows how God might use us for His Church through the whole world! Is it not worth while to sacrifice everything, and to beseech God without ceasing to give us real and full victory over the prayerlessness which has covered us with such shame?

Why do I now write these things and extol so highly the blessedness of victory over "the sin which doth so easily beset us" and which has so terribly robbed us of the power which God has intended for us? I can give an answer. I know all too well what low thoughts we have concerning the promises and the power of God and how prone we are always to backslide, to limit God's power, and to deem it impossible for Him to do greater things than we have seen. It is a glorious thing to get to know God in a new way in the inner chamber. That, however, is but the beginning. It is something still greater and more glorious to know God as the All-sufficient One and to wait on His Spirit to open our hearts and minds wide to receive the great things, the new things which He really longs to bestow on those who wait for Him.

God's object is to encourage faith and to make His children and servants see that they must take trouble to understand and rely upon the unspeakable greatness and omnipotence of God, so that they may take literally and in a childlike spirit this word: "Unto him that is able to do exceeding abundantly above all that we ask or think . . . be glory throughout all ages" (Eph. 3:20, 21). Oh, that we knew what a great and glorious God we have!

Someone may ask: "May not this note of certain victory become a snare and lead to levity and pride?" Undoubtedly. That which is the highest and best on earth is always liable to abuse. How, then, can we be saved from this? Through nothing so surely as through true prayer, which brings us really into contact with God. The holiness of God, sought for in persistent prayer, will cover our sinfulness. The omnipotence and greatness of God will make us feel our nothingness. Fellowship with God in Jesus Christ will lead us to the experience that there is in us no good thing, and that we can have fellowship with God only as our faith becomes a humbling of ourselves as Christ humbled Himself, and we truly live in Him as He is in the Father.

Prayer is not merely coming to God to ask something from Him. *It is above all fellowship with God and being brought under the power of His holiness and love,* till He takes possession of us and stamps our entire nature with the lowliness of Christ, which is the secret of all true worship.

Yes, it is in Christ Jesus that we draw near to the Father, as those who have died with Christ and have entirely done with their own life, as those in whom He lives and whom He enables to say: "Christ liveth in me." What we have said about the work that the Lord Jesus does in us to deliver us from prayerlessness is true not only of the beginning of the life of prayer, and of the joy which a new experience of power to pray causes us, it is true for the whole life of prayer all the day long. *"Through him"* we have access to the Father. In this always, as in the whole spiritual life, "Christ is all." "They saw no man save Jesus only."

May God strengthen us to a belief that there is certain victory prepared for us, and that the blessing will be what the heart of man has not conceived! God will do this for those who love Him.

This does not come to us all at once. God has great patience with His children. He bears with us in our slow progress with Fatherly patience. Let each child of God rejoice in all that God's Word promises. The stronger our faith, the more earnestly will we persevere to the end.

The More Abundant Life

Our Lord spoke this word concerning the more abundant life when He said that He had come to give His life for His sheep: "I am come that they might have life, and that they might have it more abundantly" (John 10:10). A man may have life, and yet, through lack of nourishment, or through illness, there may be no abundance of life or power. This was the distinction between the Old Testament and the New. In the former there was indeed life, under the law, but not the abundance of grace of the New Testament. Christ had given life to His disciples, but they could receive the abundant life only through His resurrection and the gift of the Holy Spirit.

All true Christians have received life from Christ. The greater portion of them, however, know nothing about the more abundant life which He is willing to bestow. Paul speaks constantly of this. He says about himself that the grace of God was "exceeding abundant": "I can do all things through Christ who strengtheneth me." "Thanks be unto God, who always causeth us to triumph in Christ." "We are more than conquerors through him that loved us."

We have spoken of the sin of prayerlessness, and the means of deliverance, and how to be kept free from this sin. What has been said on these points is all included in that expression of Christ: "I am come that they might have life, and that they might have it more abundantly." It is of the utmost importance for us so to understand this more abundant life, that we may clearly see that for a true life of prayer nothing less is necessary than that we should walk in an ever increasing experience of that overflowing life.

It is possible for us to commence this conflict against prayerlessness in dependence on Christ, and looking to Him to be assisted and kept in it, and yet to be disappointed. This is the case when prayerlessness is looked upon as the one sin against which we must strive. It must be recognized as part of the whole life of the flesh and as closely connected with other sins which spring from the same source. We forget that the entire flesh with all its affections, whether manifested in the body or soul, must be regarded as crucified and be handed over to death. We must not be satisfied with a feeble life, but must seek for an abundant life. We must surrender ourselves entirely, that the Spirit may take full possession of us, so manifesting that life in us that there may come an entire transformation in our spiritual being, by which the complete mastery of Christ and the Spirit is recognized.

What is it, then, which peculiarly constitutes this abundant life? We cannot too often repeat, or in different ways too often set it forth—the abundant life is nothing less than *the full Jesus having the full mastery over our entire being, through the power of the Holy Spirit*. As the Spirit makes known in us the fullness of Christ, and the abundant life which He gives, it will be chiefly in three aspects:—

1. AS THE CRUCIFIED ONE.—Not merely as the

51

One who died for us, to atone for our sins; but as He *who has taken us up with Himself on the cross to die with Him,* and who now works out in us the power of His cross and death. You have the true fellowship with Christ when you can say: "I have been crucified with Christ—He, the Crucified One, lives in me." *The feelings and the disposition which were in Him,* His lowliness and obedience even to the death of the cross—these were what He referred to when He said of the Holy Spirit: "He shall take of mine, and shall show it unto you"—not as an instruction, but as childlike participation of the same life which was in Him.

Do you desire that the Holy Spirit should take full possession of you, so as to cause *the crucified Christ to dwell in you?* Understand then, that this is just the end for which He has been given, and this He will surely accomplish in all who yield themselves to Him.

2. As the risen One.—The Scripture frequently mentions the resurrection in connection with the wonder-working power of God, by which Christ was raised from the dead; and from which comes the assurance of *"the exceeding greatness of his power to us-ward who believe,* according to the working of his mighty power which he wrought in Christ, when he raised him from the dead" (Eph. 1:19, 20). Do not pass hastily from these words. Turn back and read them once more, and learn the

great lesson that, however powerless and weak you feel, the omnipotence of God *is working in you;* and, if you only believe, will give you in daily life a share in the resurrection of His Son.

Yes, the Holy Spirit can fill you with the joy and victory of the resurrection of Christ, as the power of your daily life, here in the midst of the trials and temptations of this world. Let the cross humble you to death. God will work out the heavenly life in you through His Spirit. Ah, how little have we understood that it is entirely the work of the Holy Spirit to make us partakers of the crucified and risen Christ, and to conform us to His life and death!

3. AS THE GLORIFIED ONE—The glorified Christ is He who baptizes with the Holy Spirit. When the Lord Jesus Himself was baptized with the Spirit, it was because He had humbled Himself and offered Himself to take part in John's baptism of repentance—a baptism for sinners—in Jordan. Even so, when He took upon Himself the work of redemption, He received the Holy Spirit to fit Him for His work from that hour till on the cross "he offered himself without spot to God." Do you desire that this glorified Christ should baptize you with the Holy Spirit? Offer yourself then to Him for His service, to further His great work of making known to sinners the love of the Father.

God help us to understand what a great thing

it is *to receive the Holy Spirit with power from the glorified Jesus!* It means a willingness—a longing of the soul—to work for Him, and, if need be, to suffer for Him. You have known and loved your Lord, and have worked for Him, and have had blessing in that work; but the Lord has more than that to bestow. He can so work in us, and in our brethren around us, and in the ministers of the Church, by the power of the Holy Spirit, as to fill our hearts with adoring wonder.

Have you laid hold of it, my reader? The abundant life is neither more nor less than the full life of Christ as the crucified, the risen, the glorified One, who baptizes with the Holy Ghost and reveals Himself in our hearts and lives as Lord of all within us.

I read not long since an expression—"Live in what must be." Do not live in your human imagination of what is possible. *Live in the Word—in the love and infinite faithfulness of the Lord Jesus.* Even though it is slow, and with many a stumble, the faith that always thanks Him—not for experiences, but for the promises on which it can rely—goes on from strength to strength, still increasing in the blessed assurance that God Himself will perfect His work in us.

5

THE EXAMPLE OF OUR LORD

THE CONNECTION between the prayer life and the Spirit life is close and indissoluble. It is not merely that we can receive the Spirit through prayer, but the Spirit life requires, as an indispensable thing, a continuous prayer life. I can be led continually by the Spirit only as I continually give myself to prayer.

This was very evident in the life of our Lord. A study of His life will give us a wonderful view of the power and holiness of prayer.

Consider His baptism. It was when He was baptized and prayed that heaven was opened and the Holy Spirit came down upon Him. God desired to crown Christ's surrender of Himself to the sinner's baptism in Jordan (which was also a surrender of Himself to the sinner's death), with the gift of the Spirit for the work that He must accomplish. *But this could not have taken place had He not prayed.* In the fellowship of worship the Spirit was bestowed on Him to lead Him out into the desert to spend forty days there in prayer and fasting. Turn to Mark 1:32-35: "And at even, when the sun did set, they brought unto him all that were diseased, and them that were possessed with devils. And all the city was gathered together at the door. . . . And in the morning, rising up a great while before day, he went out, and departed into a solitary place, and there prayed."

The work of the day and evening had exhausted Him. In His healing of the sick and casting out devils, power had gone out of Him. While others still slept, He went away to pray and *to renew His strength in communion with His Father*. He had need of this, otherwise He would not have been ready for the new day. The holy work of delivering souls demands constant renewal through fellowship with God.

Think again of the calling of the apostles as given in Luke 6:12, 13: "And it came to pass in those days, that He went out into a mountain to pray, and *continued all night in prayer to God*. And when it was day, he called unto him his disciples: and of them he choose twelve, whom also he named apostles." Is it not clear that if anyone wishes to do God's work, *he must take time for fellowship with Him, to receive His wisdom and power?* The dependence and helplessness of which this is an evidence, open the way and give God the opportunity of revealing His power. How great was the importance of the choosing of the apostles for Christ's own work, for the Early Church, and for all time! It had God's blessing and seal; the stamp of prayer was on it.

Read Luke 9:18, 20: "And it came to pass, as he was *alone praying,* his disciples were with him: and he asked them saying, Whom say the people that I am? . . . Peter answering said, The Christ of God." The Lord had intended that the Father might reveal to them who He was, and for this purpose He had chosen the twelve apostles (see John 17:6-8). After a night of prayer, "he chose twelve, whom also he named apostles" (Luke 6:12-13). It was one of these, Peter, who said, "Thou art the Christ," the Son of the living God"; and the Lord then said, "Flesh and blood hath not revealed it unto thee, but my Father which is in heaven" (Mat. 16:16-17). This great confession was the fruit of prayer.

Read further Luke 9:28-35: "He took Peter and John and James, and *went up into a mountain to pray.* And *as he prayed,* the fashion of his countenance was altered . . . and there came a voice out of the cloud, saying, This is my beloved Son, hear him." Christ had desired that, for the strengthening of their faith, God might give them an assurance from heaven that He was the Son of God. Prayer obtained for our Lord Jesus Himself, as well as for

His disciples, what happened on the Mount of Transfiguration.

Does it not become still more clear that *what God wills to accomplish on earth needs prayer as its indispensable condition?* And there is but one way for Christ and believers. A heart and mouth open toward heaven in believing prayer will certainly not be put to shame.

Read Luke 11:1-13: "As he was *praying* in a certain place, when he ceased, one of his disciples said unto him, Lord, *teach us to pray . . .* " And then He gave them that inexhaustible prayer: "Our Father who art in heaven." In this He showed what was going on in His heart, when He prayed that God's name might be hallowed, and His kingdom come, and His will be done, and all of this "on earth as it is in heaven." How will this ever come to pass? Through prayer. This prayer has been uttered through the ages by countless millions, to their unspeakable comfort. But forget not this—it was born out of the prayer of our Lord Jesus. He had been praying, and therefore was able to give that glorious answer.

Read John 14:16: "I will *pray* the Father, and he shall give you another Comforter." The entire dispensation of the New Testament, with the wonderful outpouring of the Holy Spirit, is the outcome of the prayer of the Lord Jesus. It is as though God had impressed on the gift of the Holy Spirit this seal—in answer to the prayer of the Lord Jesus, and later of His disciples, the Holy Spirit will surely come. But it will be in answer to prayer like that of our Lord, *in which He took time to be alone with God and in that prayer offered Himself wholly to God.*

Read John 17, the high priestly, most holy prayer! Here the Son prays first for Himself, that the Father will glorify Him by giving Him power for the Cross, by raising Him from the dead, by setting Him at His right hand. These great things could not take place save through prayer. Prayer had power to obtain them.

Afterward He prayed for His disciples, that the Father might preserve them from the evil one, might keep them from the world, and might sanctify them. And then, further, He prayed for all those who through their word might believe on Him, that all might be one in love, even as the Father and the Son were One. This prayer gives us a glimpse into the wonderful relationship between the Father and the Son, and teaches us that all the blessings of heaven come continually through the prayer of Him who is at God's right hand and ever prays for us. But it teaches us, also, that all these blessings must in the same manner be desired and asked for by us. The whole nature and glory of God's blessings consist in this—they must be obtained *in answer to prayer,* by hearts entirely surrendered to Him, and hearts that believe in the power of prayer.

Now we come to the most remarkable instance of all. In Gethsemane we see that our Lord, according to His constant habit, consulted and arranged with the Father the work He had to do on earth. First He besought Him in agony and bloody sweat to let the cup pass from Him; when He understood that this could not be, then He prayed for strength to drink it, and surrendered Himself with the words: "Thy will be done." He was able to meet the enemy full of courage and in the power of God gave Himself over to the death of the cross. *He had prayed.*

Oh, why is it that God's children have so little faith in the glory of prayer, as the great power for subjecting our own wills to that of God, as well as for the confident carrying out of the work of God in spite of our great weakness? Would that we might learn from our Lord Jesus how impossible it is to walk with God, to obtain God's blessing or leading, or to do His work joyously and fruitfully, apart from close unbroken fellowship with Him who is ever a living fountain of spiritual life and power!

Let every Christian think over this simple study of the prayer life of our Lord Jesus and endeavor from God's Word, with prayer for the leading of the Holy Spirit, *to learn what the life is which the Lord Jesus Christ bestows upon him and supports in him*. It is nothing else than a life of daily prayer. Let each minister especially recognize how entirely vain it is to attempt to do the work of our Lord in any other way than that in which He did it. Let us, as workers, begin to believe that we are set free from the ordinary business of the world, that we may, above everything, have time, in our Saviour's name, and with His Spirit, and in oneness with Him, to *ask for and obtain blessing for the world*.

6

THE HOLY SPIRIT AND PRAYER

Is it not sad that our thoughts about the Holy Spirit are so often coupled with grief and self-reproach? Yet He bears the name of Comforter, and is given to lead us to find in Christ our chief delight and joy. But there is something still more sad: He who dwells within us to comfort us is often grieved by us because we will not permit Him to accomplish His work of love. What a cause of inexpressible pain to the Holy Spirit is all this prayerlessness in the Church! It is the cause also of the low vitality and utter impotence which are so often found in us, because we are not prepared to permit the Holy Spirit to lead us.

God grant that our meditation on the work of the Holy Spirit may be matter for rejoicing and for the strengthening of our faith!

The Holy Spirit is "the Spirit of prayer." He is definitely called by this name in Zechariah 12:10:

"The spirit of grace and of supplications." Twice in Paul's Epistles there is a remarkable reference to Him in the matter of prayer. "Ye have received the Spirit of adoption, WHEREBY WE CRY, Abba, Father" (Rom. 8:15). "God hath sent forth the Spirit of his Son into your hearts, crying, Abba, Father" (Gal. 4:6). Have you ever meditated on these words: "Abba, Father"? In that name our Saviour offered His greatest prayer to the Father, accompanied by the entire surrender and sacrifice of His life and love. *The Holy Spirit is given for the express purpose* of teaching us, from the very beginning of our Christian life onward, to utter that word in childlike trust and surrender. In one of these passages we read: "We cry"; in the other: "He cries." What a wonderful blending of the divine and human co-operation in prayer. What a proof that God—if I may say so—has done His utmost to make prayer as natural and effectual as though it were the cry of a child to an earthly Father, as he says: "Abba, Father."

Is it not a proof that the Holy Spirit is to a great extent a stranger in the Church, when prayer, for which God has made such provisions, is regarded as a task and a burden? And does not this teach us to seek for the deep root of prayerlessness in our ignorance of, and disobedience to, the divine Instructor whom the Father has commissioned to teach us to pray?

If we desire to understand this truth still more clearly we must notice what is written in Romans 8:26, 27: "Likewise the Spirit also helpeth our infirmities: for we know not what we should pray for as we ought: but the Spirit himself maketh intercession for us, with groanings which cannot be uttered. And he that searcheth the hearts knoweth what is the mind of the Spirit, because he maketh intercession for the saints according to the will of God." Is it not clear from this that the Christian if left to himself does not know how to pray; or how he ought to pray; and that God has stooped to meet us in this helplessness of ours by giving us the Holy Spirit Himself to pray for us; and that His operation is deeper than our thought or feeling, but is noticed and answered by God?

Our first work, therefore, ought to be to come into God's presence not with our ignorant prayers, not with many words and thoughts, but in the confidence that the divine work of the Holy Spirit is being carried on within us. This confidence will encourage reverence and quietness, and will also enable us, in dependence on the help which the Spirit gives, to lay our desires and heart-needs before God. The great lesson for every prayer is—see to it, first of all, that you commit yourself to the leading of the Holy Spirit, and with entire dependence on Him, give Him the first place; for through Him your prayer will have a value you cannot imagine, and through Him also you will learn to speak out your desires in the name of Christ.

What a protection this faith would be against deadness and despondency in the inner chamber! Only think of it! In every prayer the Triune God takes a part—the Father who hears; the Son in whose name we pray; the Spirit who prays for us and in us. How important it is that we should be in right relationship to the Holy Spirit and understand His work!

The following points demand serious consideration.

1. Let us firmly believe, as a divine reality, that *the Spirit of God's Son, the Holy Spirit, is in us.* Do not imagine that you know this and have no need to consider it. It is a thought so great and divine that it can gain an entrance to our hearts and be retained there only by the Holy Spirit Himself. "The Spirit beareth witness with our spirit." Our position ought to be that of reckoning with full assurance of faith that our heart is His temple, yes, that He dwells within us and rules soul and body. Let us thank God heartily as often as we pray, that we have His Spirit in us to teach us to pray. Thanksgiving will draw our hearts out to God and keep us engaged with Him; it will take our attention from ourselves and give the Spirit room in our hearts.

Oh, it is no wonder that we have been prayerless, and have felt this work too heavy for us, if we have sought to hold fellowship with the Eternal God apart from His Spirit, who reveals the Father and the Son.

2. In the practice of this faith in the certainty that the Spirit dwells and works in us, there must also be *the understanding of all that He desires to accomplish in us.* His work in prayer is closely connected with His other work. We have seen in an earlier chapter that His first and greatest work is to reveal Christ in His omnipresent love and power. So the Holy Spirit will in prayer constantly remind us of Christ, of His blood and name, as the sure ground of our being heard.

He will, further, as "the Spirit of holiness," teach us to recognize, and hate, and have done with sin. He is "the Spirit of light and wisdom" who leads us into the heavenly secret of God's overflowing grace. He is "the Spirit of love and power" who teaches us to witness for Christ and to labor for souls with tender pity. The more closely I associate all these blessings with the Spirit, the more shall I be convinced of His deity and shall be the more ready to commit myself to His guidance, as I give myself to prayer. What a different life mine would be if I *knew* the Spirit as the Spirit of prayer! There is still another thing which I need constantly to learn afresh, that—

3. THE SPIRIT DESIRES TO HAVE FULL POSSES-

SION OF MY LIFE. We pray for more of the Spirit, and we pray well, if alongside this prayer we set the truth that the Spirit wants more of me. The Spirit would possess me entirely. Just as my soul has my whole body for its dwelling-place and service, *so the Holy Spirit would have my body and soul as His dwelling-place, entirely under His control.* No one can continue long and earnestly in prayer without beginning to perceive that the Spirit is gently leading to an entirely new consecration, of which previously he knew nothing. "I seek Thee with my whole heart." The Spirit will make such words more and more the motto of our lives. He will cause us to recognize that what remains in us of doublemindedness is truly sinful. He will reveal Christ as the Almighty Deliverer from all sin, who is always near to defend us. He will lead us in this way in prayer, to forget ourselves and make us willing to offer ourselves for training as intercessors, to whom God can entrust the carrying out of His plans, and who day and night cry to Him to avenge His Church of her adversary.

God help us to know the Spirit and to reverence Him as the Spirit of prayer!

7

SIN; THE HOLINESS OF GOD

To UNDERSTAND grace, to understand Christ aright, we must understand what sin is. And how otherwise can we come to this understanding than through the light of God and His Word?

Come with me to the beginning of the Bible. See there man created by God, after His image, and pronounced by his Creator to be very good. Then sin entered, as rebellion against God. Adam was driven out of paradise and was brought along with the untold millions of following generations under curse and ruin. *That was the work of sin.* Here we learn its nature and power.

Come further on and see the Ark of Noah on Ararat. So terrible had godlessness become among men, God saw nothing for it but to destroy man from off the earth. *That was the work of sin.*

Come once more with me to Sinai. God wished to establish His covenant with a new nation—with the people of Israel. But because of man's sinfulness, He could do this only by appearing in darkness and lightning so terrible that Moses said: "I exceedingly fear and quake." And before the end of the giving of the law that awful message came: "Cursed is every one that continueth not in all things that are written in the book of the law to do them." *It was sin which made that necessary.*

Come once more with me, and this time to Calvary. There see what sin is, and the hatred and enmity with which the world cast out and crucified the Son of God. *There sin reached its climax.* There Christ was, by God Himself, made sin, and became a curse, as the only way to destroy sin. In the agony in which He prayed in Gethsemane, that He might not drink the terrible cup, and in the agony in which on the cross, in the deep darkness of desertion, He cried out: "My God, my God, why hast thou forsaken me?" we obtain at least some faint idea of the curse and indescribable suffering which sin brings. If anything can make us hate and detest sin, it is Christ on the cross.

Come once again with me to the judgment seat of the Great Day, and see the bottomless pit of darkness wherein countless souls will be plunged under the sentence: "Depart from me ye cursed, into everlasting fire." Oh, will not these words soften our hearts and fill us with a never-to-be-forgotten horror of sin, so that we may hate it with a perfect hatred?

And now is there anything else that can help us

to understand what sin is? Yes, there is. Turn your eyes inward, and behold your own heart, and see sin there. Remember that all you have already seen of the hatefulness and godlessness of sin should teach you what sin in your own heart means—all the enmity against God, all the ruin of men, all of its inner nature of hatefulness, lie hidden in the sin you have committed, guilt of every transgression against God. And when you acknowledge that you are a child of God and yet commit sin, allowing it sometimes to fulfill its lusts, is it not fitting that you should cry out with shame: "Woe is me, because of my sin?" "Depart from me, for I am a sinful man, O Lord."

One great power of sin is that it blinds men so that they do not recognize its true character. Even the Christian himself finds an excuse in the thought that he can never be perfect and that daily sin is a necessity. He is so accustomed to the thought of sinning that he has almost lost the power and ability of mourning over sin. And yet there can be no real progress in grace apart from an increased consciousness of the sin and guilt of every transgression against God. And there cannot be a more important question than this: "How can I regain the lost tenderness of conscience and become prepared really to offer to God the sacrifice of a broken heart?"

Scripture teaches us the way. Let the Christian remember what God thinks about sin—the hatred with which His holiness burns against it, the solemn sacrifice which He made to conquer sin, and deliver us from it. Let him tarry in God's presence till His holiness shines upon him, and he cries out with Isaiah: "Woe is me, for I am undone!"

Let him remember the cross, and what the love of Christ had to endure there, through the unspeakable pain which sin caused Him; and let him ask if this will not teach him to hearken to the voice which says: "Oh, do not this abominable thing which I hate." Let him take time, so that the blood and love of the cross may exercise their full influence on him, and let him think of sin as nothing less than giving his hand to Satan and to his power. Is not this a terrible result of our prayerlessness, and of our short and hasty tarrying before God—that the true knowledge of sin is almost lost?

Let the believer think not only of what redemption has cost Christ, but also of the fact that Christ is offered to him, by the Holy Spirit, as a gift of inconceivable grace, through whom divine forgiveness and purification and renewing have taken possession of him; and let him ask himself with what return such love should be repaid. If only time were taken to tarry in God's presence and ask such questions, the Spirit of God would accomplish His work of conviction of sin in us and would teach us to take an entirely new standpoint, and would give us a new view of sin. The thought would begin to arise in our hearts that we have in very deed been redeemed, so that in the power of Christ we may live every day as partners in the great victory which Christ obtained over sin on the cross, and manifest it in our walk.

What think you? Do you not begin to see that the sin of prayerlessness has had a more terrible effect than you at first supposed? It is because of this hasty and superficial converse with God that the sense of sin is so weak and that no motives have power to help you to hate and flee from sin as you ought. Nothing, nothing except the hidden, humble, constant fellowship with God can teach you, as a child of God, to hate sin as God wants you to hate it. Nothing, nothing but the constant nearness and unceasing power of the living Christ can make it possible for you rightly to understand what sin is and to detest it. And without this deeper understanding of sin, there will be no thought of appropriating the victory which is made possible for you in Christ Jesus, and will be wrought in you by the Spirit.

O my God, cause me to know my sin and teach me to tarry before Thee and to wait on Thee till Thy Spirit causes something of Thy holiness to rest upon me! O my God, cause me to know my sin, and let this drive me to listen to the promise: "He that abideth in him sinneth not," and to expect the fulfillment from Thee!

THE HOLINESS OF GOD

IT HAS OFTEN been said that the conception of sin and of the holiness of God has been lost in the Church. In the inner chamber we have the place where we may learn again how to give God's holiness the position it should have in our faith and life. If you do not know how to spend half an hour in prayer, take up the subject of God's holiness. Bow before Him. Give yourself time, and give God also time, that He and you may come into touch with one another. It is a great work, but one fraught with great blessing.

If you wish to strengthen yourself in the practice of this Holy Presence, take up the Holy Word. Take, for instance, the Book of Leviticus and notice how God seven times gives the command: "Ye shall be holy, for I am holy" (11:44, 45; 19:2; 20:7, 26; 21:8; 22:32). Still more frequent is the expression: "I am the Lord that doth sanctify you." This great thought is taken over into the New Testament. Peter says (I Peter 1:15, 16): "Be ye holy in all manner of conversation; because it is written, Be ye holy, for I am holy." Paul writes in his first epistle (I Thess. 3:13; 4:7; 5:24): "That he may stablish your hearts unblameable in holiness. . . . God hath called us unto holiness. . . . *Faithful is he that calleth you, who also will do it.*"

Nothing but the knowledge of God, as the Holy

One, will make us holy. And how are we to obtain that knowledge of God, save in the inner chamber? It is a thing utterly impossible unless we take time and allow the holiness of God to shine on us. How can any man on earth obtain intimate knowledge of another man of remarkable wisdom, if he does not associate with him, and place himself under his influence? And how can God Himself sanctify us, if we do not take time to be brought under the power of the glory of His holiness? Nowhere can we get to know the holiness of God, and come under its influence and power, *save in the inner chamber*. It has been well said: "No man can expect to make progress in holiness who is not *often and long alone with God.*"

And what now is this holiness of God? It is the highest and most glorious and most all-embracing of all the attributes of God. Holiness is the most profound word in the Bible. It is a word that is at home in heaven. Both the Old and New Testaments tell us this. Isaiah heard the seraphs with veiled faces cry out: "Holy, holy, holy, is the Lord of hosts" (6:3). John heard the four living creatures say: "Holy, holy, holy, Lord God Almighty" (Rev. 4:8). This is the highest expression of God's glory in heaven, by beings who live in His immediate presence and bow low before Him. And dare we imagine that we, by thinking, and reading, and hearing, can understand or become partakers of the holiness of God? What folly! Oh, that we might begin to thank God that we have a place in the inner chamber, a place where we can be alone with Him, and take time for the prayer: "Let Thy holiness, O Lord, shine more and more into our hearts, that they may become holy."

And let our hearts be deeply ashamed of our prayerlessness, through which we have made it impossible for God to impart His holiness to us. Let us beseech God fervently to forgive us this sin, and to allure us by His heavenly grace, and to strengthen us to have fellowship with Him, the holy God.

I have said that the meaning of the words, "The holiness of God," is not easily expressed. But we may begin by saying that they imply the unspeakable aversion and hatred with which God regards sin. And if you wish to understand what that means, remember that He preferred to see His Son die, rather than that sin should reign. Think of the Son of God, who gave up His life rather than act in the least matter against the will of the Father. Still further, He had such a hatred of sin that He preferred to die rather than that men should be held in its power. That is something of the holiness of God, which is a pledge that He will do everything for us —for you and me—to deliver us from sin. Holiness is the fire of God that will consume sin in us and make us holy sacrifices, pure and acceptable before Him. It was for this reason that the Spirit came down as fire. He is the Spirit of God's holiness, the Spirit of sanctification in us.

Oh, think over the holiness of God, and bow in lowliness before Him, till your heart is filled with the assurance of what the Holy One will do for you. Take a week, if necessary, to read and re-read the words of God on this great truth, till your heart is brought under the conviction: *"This is the glory of the inner chamber, to converse with God the Holy One;* to bow in deep humility and shame before Him, because we have so despised Him and His love through our prayerlessness." There we shall receive the assurance that He will again take us into fellowship with Himself. No one can expect to understand and receive the holiness of God who is not *often and long alone with God.*

Someone has said that the holiness of God is the expression of the unspeakable distance by which He in His righteousness is separated from us, and yet also of the unspeakable nearness in which He in His love longs to hold fellowship with us and dwell in us. Bow in humble reverence, as you think of the immeasurable distance between you and God. Bow in childlike confidence in the unspeakable desire of His love to be united with you in the deepest intimacy; and reckon most confidently on Him to reveal something of His holiness to the soul which thirsts after Him and waits upon Him and is quiet before Him.

Notice how the two sides of the holiness of God are united in the cross. So terrible was the aversion and anger of God against our sin that Christ was left in the thick darkness, because God, when sin was laid upon Him, had to hide His face from Him. And yet so deep was the love of God toward us and He so desired to be united to us that He spared not His Son but gave Him over to unutterable sufferings, that so He might receive us, in union with Christ, into His holiness, and press us to His heart as His beloved children. It was of this suffering that our Lord Jesus said: "I sanctify myself, that they also might be sanctified through the truth" (John 17:19). Thus He is become of God our sanctification, and we are holy in Him.

I beseech you, think not little of the grace that you have a holy God who longs to make you holy. Think not little of the voice of God which calls you to give time to Him in the stillness of the inner chamber, so that He may cause His holiness to rest on you. Let it be your business every day, in the secrecy of the inner chamber, to meet the holy God. You will be repaid for the trouble it may cost you. The reward will be sure and rich. You will learn to hate sin, and to regard it as accursed and conquered. The new nature will give you a horror of sin. The living Jesus, the holy God, will, as Conqueror, be your power and strength; and you will begin to believe the great promise contained in I

Thessalonians 5: 23, 24: "The very God of peace sanctify you wholly. . . . Faithful is he that calleth you, who also will do it."

8

OBEDIENCE;
THE VICTORIOUS LIFE

IN OPPOSITION to sin stands obedience. "For as by one man's disobedience many were made sinners, so by the obedience of one shall many be made righteous. . . . Ye became the servants of righteousness" (Rom. 5:19; 6:18). In connection with all that has been said about sin, and the new life, and the reception of the Holy Spirit, we must always give to obedience the place assigned to it by God.

It was because Christ humbled Himself and became *obedient* unto death, yea, the death of the cross, that God so highly exalted Him. And Paul, in this connection, exhorts us: "Let this mind be in you which was also in Christ Jesus" (Phil. 2:5). We see, above everything else, that the obedience of Christ, which was so pleasing to God, must become really the characteristic of our disposition and of our entire walk. Just as a servant knows that he must first obey his master in all things, so *the surrender to an implicit and unquestionable obedience must become the essential characteristic of our lives.*

How little this is understood by Christians! How many there are who allow themselves to be misled, and rest satisfied with the thought that sin is a necessity, that one must sin every day! It would be difficult to say how great the harm is which has been done by this mistake. It is one of the chief causes why the sin of disobedience is so little recognized. I have myself heard Christians, speaking about the cause of darkness and weakness, say, half-laughingly: "Yes, it is just disobedience again." We try to get rid of a servant as speedily as possible who is habitually disobedient, but it is not regarded as anything extraordinary that a child of God should be disobedient every day. Disobedience is daily acknowledged, and yet there is no turning away from it.

Have we not here the reason why so much prayer for the power of the Holy Spirit is offered, and yet so few answers come? Do we not read that "God has given his Holy Spirit to them that obey him"? Every child of God has received the Holy Spirit. If he uses the measure of the Holy Spirit which he has, with the definite purpose of being obedient to the utmost, then God can and will favor him with further manifestations of the Spirit's power. But if he permits disobedience to get the upper hand, day by day, he need not wonder if his prayer for more of the Spirit remains unanswered.

We have already said that we must not forget that the Spirit desires to possess more of us. How can we wholly surrender ourselves to Him otherwise than by being obedient? The Scripture says that we must be led by the Spirit, that we must walk by the Spirit. My right relationship to the Holy Spirit is that I allow myself to be guided and ruled by Him. Obedience is the great factor in our whole relationship to God. "Obey My voice, and I will be your God."

Mark how the Lord Jesus, on the last night, when giving His great promise about the Holy Spirit, lays emphasis on this point. "If ye love me, *keep my commandments.* And I will pray the Father, and he shall give you another Comforter" (John 14:15, 16). Obedience was essential as a preparation for the reception of the Spirit. And this thought is often repeated by Him. "He that hath my commandments, and *keepeth them,* he it is that loveth me: and he that loveth me shall be loved of my Father, and I will love him, and will manifest myself to him" (John 14:21). So also in verse 23: "If a man love me, he *will keep my words:* and my Father will love him, and we will come unto him, and make our abode with him." "If ye abide in me, and *my words abide in you,* ye shall ask what ye will, and it shall be done unto you" (15:7). "If ye *keep my commandments,* ye shall abide in my love" (verse 10). "Ye are my friends, if *ye do whatsoever I command you*" (verse 14).

Can words more plainly or impressively declare that the whole life, in the new dispensation, following the resurrection of Christ, depends on obedience? That is the Spirit of Christ. He lived to do not His own will, but the will of the Father. And He cannot with His Spirit make an abiding home in the heart of one who does not surrender himself utterly to a life of obedience.

Alas, how few there are who are truly concerned because of this disobedience! How little it is believed that Christ really asks for and expects this from us—because He has undertaken to make it possible for us. How much is it manifested in prayer, or walk, or in the depths of the soul-life, that we really endeavor to be well-pleasing to the Lord in all things? We say too little in regard to our disobedience. "I will be sorry for my sin."

But is obedience really possible? It is certain for the man who believes that Christ Jesus is his sanctification and relies on Him.

Just as it is impossible for a man whose eyes have not yet been opened to see that Christ can at once forgive his sin, so is it also with faith in the assurance that there is in Christ a sure promise of power to accomplish all that God desires from His child. Just as, through faith, we found the fullness of forgiveness; so through a new act of faith, a real deliverance from the dominion of the sin which has so easily beset us is obtained, and the abiding blessing of the continuous experience of the keeping power of Christ becomes ours. This faith obtains a new insight into promises the meaning of which was not previously understood: "The God of peace . . . *make you perfect in every good work to do his will,* working in you that which is well pleasing in his sight, through Jesus Christ" (Heb. 13:20, 21). "Unto him that is able to keep you from falling . . . be glory and majesty" (Jude 24, 25). "Give diligence to make your calling and election sure: for if ye do these things, ye shall never fall" (II Peter 1:10). "To the end he may stablish your hearts unblamable in holiness" (I Thess. 3:13). "But the Lord is faithful, who shall stablish you, and keep you from evil" (II Thess. 3:3).

When the soul understands that the fulfillment of these and other promises is secured for us in Christ, and that, as certainly as the forgiveness of sin is assured to us in Him, so also is power against new or fresh attacks of sin assured to us. Then for the first time is the lesson learned aright that faith can confidently rely upon a full Christ and His abiding protection.

This faith sheds a wholly new light on the life of obedience. *Christ holds Himself responsible to work this out in me every moment if I only trust Him for it.* Then I begin to understand the important phrase with which Paul begins and closes his Epistle to the Romans (Rom. 1:5; 16:26): "The obedience of faith." Faith brings me to the Lord Jesus, not only to obtain the forgiveness of sin, but also that I may every moment enjoy the power which will make it possible for me, as a child of God, to abide in Him and to be numbered among His obedient children—of whom it is written that, as He who has called them is holy, so they also may be holy in all manner of conversation. Everything depends on whether or not I believe on the whole Christ, with the fullness of His grace that He will, not now and then but every moment, be the strength of my life. Such faith will lead to an obedience which will enable me to "walk worthy of the Lord unto *all pleasing,* being fruitful in *every good work,* strengthened with all might, according to his glorious power."

The soul which feeds on such promises will experience now, instead of the disobedience of self-effort, what the obedience of faith means. All such promises have their measure, their certainty, and their strength in the living Christ.

THE VICTORIOUS LIFE

In the chapter on "The More Abundant Life," we viewed the matter chiefly from the side of our Lord Jesus. We saw that there is to be found in him—the crucified, and the risen, and the glorified One who baptizes with the Holy Spirit—all that is needful for a life of abundant grace. In speaking of the *victorious life,* we shall now look at the matter from another standpoint. We want to see how a Christian can live really as a victor. We have already often said that the prayer life is not something which can be improved by itself. It is so intimately bound up with the entire spiritual life that it is only when that whole life (previously marked by lack of prayer) becomes renewed and sanctified that prayer can have its rightful place of power. We must not be satisfied with less than the victorious life to which God calls His children.

You remember how our Lord, in the seven epistles in the Revelation of John, concludes with a promise to those who overcome. Take the trouble of going over that seven-times repeated "him that overcometh"; and notice what unspeakably glorious promises are there given. And they were given even to churches like Ephesus, that had lost its first love; and Sardis, which "had a name to live but was dead"; and Laodicea, with her lukewarmness and self-satisfaction—as proof that, if only they would repent, they might win the crown of victory. The call comes to every Christian to strive for the crown. It is impossible to be a healthy Christian, still more impossible to be a preacher in the power of God, if everything is not sacrificed to gain the victory.

The answer to the question, as to how we attain to it, is simple. All is in Christ. "Thanks be unto

God, who always causeth us to triumph in Christ" (II Cor. 2:14). "In all these things we are more than conquerors through him that loved us" (Rom. 8:37). All depends on our right relationship to Christ, our entire surrender, perfect faith, and unbroken fellowship with Him. But you wish to know how to attain to all this. Listen once more to the simple directions as to the way by which the full enjoyment of what is prepared for you in Christ may be yours. These are—*a new discovery of sin; a new surrender to Christ; a new faith in the power which will make it possible for you to persevere.*

1. A NEW DISCOVERY OF SIN.—In Romans 3, you find described the knowledge of sin which is necessary, in repentance, for forgiveness—"That every mouth may be stopped, and all the world may become guilty before God" (verse 19). There you took your stand, you recognized your sin more or less consciously, and confessed it, and you obtained mercy. But it you would lead the victorious life, something more is needful. This comes with the experience that in you, that is, in your flesh, there dwelleth no good thing (Rom. 7:8). You have a delight in the law of God after the inner man, but you see another law in your members bringing you into captivity to the law of sin and compelling you to cry out: "O, wretched man that I am! who shall deliver me from the body of this death?" (verses 23, 24). It is not, as it was at con-

version, when you thought over your few or many sins. This work goes much deeper. You find that, as a Christian, you have no power to do the good that you wish to do. You must be brought to a new and deeper insight into the sin of your nature and into your utter weakness, even though you are a Christian, to live as you ought. And you will learn to cry out: "Who shall deliver me; I, wretched man, a prisoner bound under the law of sin?"

The answer to this question is: "I thank God through Jesus Christ our Lord." Then follows the revelation of what there is in Christ. It is not just as given in Romans 3. It is more: "I am in Christ Jesus, and the law of the Spirit of life in Christ Jesus hath made me free from the law of sin and death," under which I was bound. It is the experience that the law or power of the life of the Spirit in Christ has made me free and now calls on me, in a new sense and by a new surrender, to acknowledge Christ as the Bestower of the victory.

2. A NEW SURRENDER TO CHRIST.—You may have used these words "surrender" and "consecration" many times, but without rightly understanding what they mean. As you have been brought by the teaching of Romans 7 to a complete sense of the hopelessness of leading a true Christian life, or a true prayer life, by your own efforts, so you feel that the *Lord Jesus must take you up, by His own power, in an entirely new way; and must*

take possession of you, by His Spirit, in an entirely new measure. This alone can preserve you from constantly sinning afresh. This only can make you really victorious. This leads you to look away from yourself, really to get free from yourself, *and to expect everything from the Lord Jesus.*

If we begin to understand this, we are prepared to admit that in our nature there is nothing good, that it is under a curse, and is nailed with Christ to His cross. We come to see what Paul means when he says that we are dead to sin by the death of Christ. Thus do we obtain a share of the glorious resurrection life there is in Him. By such an insight we are encouraged to believe that Christ, through His life in us, through His continual indwelling, can keep us. Just as, at our conversion, we had no rest till we knew He had received us— so now we feel the need of coming to Him, *to receive from Him the assurance that He has really undertaken to keep us by the power of His resurrection life.* And we feel then that there must be an act as definite as His reception of us at conversion, by which He gives us the assurance of victory. And although it appears to us to be too great and too much, yet the man who casts himself, without plea, into the arms of Christ will experience that He does indeed receive us into such a fellowship as will make us, from the beginning onwards, "more than conquerors."

3. A NEW FAITH IN THE POWER WHICH WILL MAKE IT POSSIBLE FOR YOU TO PERSEVERE IN YOUR SURRENDER.—You have heard of Keswick, and the truth for which it stands. It is that *Christ is prepared to take upon Himself the care and preservation of our lives every day, and all the day long, if we trust Him to do it.* In the testimony given by many, this thought is emphasized. They have told us that they felt themselves called to a new surrender, to an entire consecration of life to Christ, reaching to the smallest things, but they were hindered by the fear of failure. The thirst after holiness, after an unbroken fellowship with Jesus, after a life of persevering childlike obedience, drew them one way. But the question arose: "Shall I continue faithful?" And to this question there came no answer, till they believed that the surrender must be made, not in their own strength, but *in a power which was bestowed by a glorified Lord.* He would not only keep them for the future, but He must first make possible for them the surrender of faith which expects that future grace. It was in the power of Christ Himself that they were able to present themselves to Him.

O Christian, only believe that there is a victorious life! Christ, the Victor, is your Lord, who will undertake for you in everything and will enable you to do all that the Father expects from you. Be of good courage. Will you not trust Him to do this great work for you who has given His life for you and has forgiven your sins? Only dare, in His power, to surrender yourself to the life of those who are kept from sin by the power of God. Along with the deepest conviction that there is no good in you, confess that you see in the Lord Jesus all the goodness of which you have need, for the life of a child of God; and begin literally to live "by the faith of the Son of God, who loved you, and gave himself for you."

Let me, for your encouragement, give the testimony of Bishop Moule, a man of deep humility and tender piety. When he first heard of Keswick he was afraid of "perfectionism" and would have nothing to do with it. Unexpectedly, during a vacation in Scotland, he came in contact with some friends at a small convention. There he heard an address by which he was convinced how entirely the teaching was according to Scripture. There was no word about sinlessness in the flesh or in man. It was a setting forth of how Jesus can keep from sin a man with a sinful nature. The light shone into his heart. He who had always been counted a tender Christian came into touch now with a new experience of what Christ is willing to do for one who gives himself entirely to Him.

Listen to what he says on the text: "I can do all things through Christ who strengtheneth me." "I dare to say that it is possible for those who really are willing to reckon on the power of the Lord, for keeping and victory, to lead a life in which His promises are taken as they stand, and are found to be true. It is possible to cast all our care on Him daily, and to enjoy deep peace in doing it. It is possible to have the thoughts and imaginations of our hearts purified in the deepest meaning of the word, through faith. It is possible to see the will of God in everything, and to receive it, not with sighing, but with singing. It is possible, in the inner life of desire and feeling, to lay aside all bitterness, and wrath, and anger, and evil-speaking, every day and every hour. It is possible, by taking complete refuge in divine power, to become strong through and through; and where previously our greatest weakness lay, to find that the things which formerly upset all our resolves to be patient, or pure, or humble, furnish today an opportunity—through Him who loved us, and works in us an agreement with His will, and a blessed sense of His presence and His power—to make sin powerless. These things are divine possibilities, and because they are His work, the true experience of them will always cause us to bow lower at His feet and to learn to thirst and long for more. We cannot possibly be satisfied with anything less than—each day, each hour, each moment, in Christ, through the power of the Holy Spirit—to walk with God.''

Thank God, a life of victory is sure for those

who have a knowledge of their inward ruin and are hopeless in themselves, but who, in "the confidence of despair," have looked to Jesus, and in faith in His power to make the act of surrender possible for them, they have done it, in His might, and now rely on Him alone every day and every hour.

9

HINTS FOR THE INNER CHAMBER; TIME

AT THE CONFERENCE, a brother who had earnestly confessed his neglect of prayer, but who was able, later, to declare that his eyes had been opened to see that the Lord really supplied grace for all that He required from us, asked if some hints could not be given as to the best way of spending time profitably in the inner chamber. There was no opportunity then for giving an answer. Perhaps the following thoughts may be of help:

1. As you enter the inner chamber let your first work be *to thank God for the unspeakable love which invites you to come to Him and to converse freely with Him.* If your heart is cold and dead, remember that religion is not a matter of feeling, but has to do first with the will. Raise your heart to God and thank Him for the assurance you have that He looks down on you and will bless you. Through such an act of faith you honor God and draw your soul away from being occupied with

itself. Think also of the glorious grace of the Lord Jesus, who is willing to teach you to pray and to give you the disposition to do so. Think, too, of the Holy Spirit who was purposely given to cry, "Abba, Father," in your heart, and to help your weakness in prayer. Five minutes spent thus will strengthen your faith for your work in the inner chamber. Once more I say, begin with an act of thanksgiving and praise God for the inner chamber and the promise of blessing there.

2. You must prepare yourself for prayer *by prayerful Bible study.* The great reason why the inner chamber is not attractive is that people do not know how to pray. Their stock of words is soon exhausted and they do not know what further to say, because they forget that prayer is not a soliloquy, where everything comes from one side; but it is a dialogue, where God's child listens to what the Father says, and replies to it, and then asks for the things he needs.

Read a few verses from the Bible. Do not concern yourself with the difficulties contained in them. You can consider these later; but take what you understand, apply it to yourself, and ask the Father to make His Word light and power in your heart. Thus you will have material enough for prayer from the Word which the Father speaks to you; you will also have the liberty to ask for things you need. Keep on in this way, and the inner chamber will become at length, not a place where you sigh and struggle only, but one of living fellowship with the Father in heaven. Prayerful study of the Bible is indispensable for powerful prayer.

3. *When you have thus received the Word into you heart, turn to prayer.* But do not attempt it hastily or thoughtlessly, as though you knew well enough how to pray. Prayer in our own strength brings no blessing. Take time to present yourself reverently and in quietness before God. Remember His greatness and holiness and love. Think over what you wish to ask from Him. Do not be satisfied with going over the same things every day. No child goes on saying the same thing day after day to his earthly father.

Converse with the Father is colored by the needs of the day. Let your prayer be something definite, arising either out of the Word which you have read, or out of the real soul-needs which you long to have satisfied. Let your prayer be so definite that you can say as you go out, "I know what I have asked from my Father, and I expect an answer." It is a good plan sometimes to take a piece of paper and write down what you wish to pray for. You might keep such a paper for a week or more, and repeat the prayers till some new need arises.

4. What has been said is in reference to your own needs. But you know that *we are allowed to pray that we may help also in the needs of others.*

One great reason why prayer in the inner chamber does not bring more joy and blessing is that it is too selfish, and selfishness is the death of prayer.

Remember your family; your congregation, with its interests; your own neighborhood; and the church to which you belong. Let your heart be enlarged and take up the interests of missions and of the church through the whole world. Become an intercessor, and you will experience for the first time the blessedness of prayer, as you find out that God will make use of you to share His blessing with others through prayer. You will begin to feel that there is something worth living for, as you find that you have something to say to God, and that He from heaven will do things in answer to your prayers which otherwise would not have been done.

A child can ask his father for bread. A full-grown son converses with him about all the interests of his business, and about his further purposes. A weak child of God prays only for himself, but a full-grown man in Christ understands how to consult with God over what must take place in the kingdom. Let your prayer list bear the names of those for whom you pray—your minister, and all other ministers, and the difference missionary affairs with which you are connected. Thus the inner chamber will really become a wonder of God's goodness and a fountain of great joy. It will become the most blessed place on earth. It is a great thing to say, but it is the simple truth, that God will make it a Bethel, where His angels shall ascend and descend, and where you will cry out: "The Lord shall be my God." He will make it also Peniel, where you will see the face of God, as a prince of God, as one who wrestled with the angel and overcame him.

5. Do not forget *the close bond between the inner chamber and the outer world*. The attitude of the inner chamber must remain with us all the day. The object of the inner chamber is so to unite us to God that we may have Him always abiding with us. Sin, thoughtlessness, and yielding to the flesh or to the world unfit us for the inner chamber and bring a cloud over the soul. If you have stumbled, or fallen, return to the inner chamber; let your first work be to invoke the blood of Jesus and to claim cleansing by it. Rest not till by confession you have repented of and put away your sin. Let the precious blood really give you a fresh freedom of approach to God. Remember that the roots of your life in the inner chamber strike far out in body and soul so as to manifest themselves in business life. Let "the obedience of faith," in which you pray in secret, rule you constantly. The inner chamber is intended to bind man to God, to supply him with power from God, to enable him to live for God alone. God be thanked for the inner

chamber and for the blessed life which He will enable us there to experience and nourish.

Time

Before the creation of the world time did not exist. God lived in eternity in a way which we little understand. With creation, time began, and everything was placed under its power. God has placed all living creatures under a law of slow growth. Think of the length of time it takes for a child to become a man in body and mind. In learning, in wisdom, in business, in handicraft, and in politics, everything somehow depends on patience and perseverance. Everything needs time.

It is just the same in religion. There can be no converse with a holy God, no fellowship between heaven and earth, no power for the salvation of the souls of others, *unless much time is set apart for it.* Just as it is necessary for a child for long years to eat and learn every day, so the life of grace entirely depends on the time men are willing to give to it day by day.

The minister is appointed by God to teach and help those who are engaged in the ordinary avocations of life to find time and to use it aright for the preservation of the spiritual life. The minister cannot do this unless he himself has a living experience of a life of prayer. His highest calling is not preaching, or speaking, or parochial visitation, but it is *to cultivate the life of God daily,* and to be a witness of what the Lord teaches him and accomplishes in him.

Was it not so with the Lord Jesus? Why must He, who had no sin to confess, sometimes spend all night in prayer to God? *Because the divine life had to be strengthened in intercourse with His Father.* His experience of a life in which He took time for fellowship with God has enabled Him to share that life with us.

Oh, that each minister might understand that he has received his time from God with a servitude on it! *God must have for fellowship with Himself the first and the best of your time.* Without this, your preaching and labor have little power. Here on earth I may spend my time for the money or the learning which I receive in exchange. The minister can exchange his time for the divine power and the spiritual blessings to be obtained from heaven. That, and nothing else, makes him a man of God and ensures that his preaching will be in the demonstration of the Spirit and power.

10

THE EXAMPLE OF PAUL

"Be ye followers of me, even as I also am of Christ." I Corinthians 11:1

1. PAUL WAS A MINISTER WHO PRAYED MUCH FOR HIS CONGREGATION.—Let us read his words prayerfully and calmly so that we may hear the voice of the Spirit.

"NIGHT AND DAY PRAYING EXCEEDINGLY that we . . . might perfect that which is lacking in your faith. . . . The Lord make you to increase . . . to the end he may stablish your hearts unblamable in holiness" (I Thess. 3:10-13).

"The very God of peace sanctify you wholly" (I Thess. 5:23).

What food for meditation!

"Now our Lord Jesus Christ himself . . . comfort your hearts, and stablish you in every good word and work" (II Thess. 2:16, 17).

"WITHOUT CEASING, I MAKE MENTION OF YOU ALWAYS IN MY PRAYERS, making request . . . that

I may impart unto you some spiritual gift, to the end ye may be established" (Rom. 1:9-11).

"My heart's desire and prayer to God for Israel is that they might be saved" (Rom. 10:1).

"I . . . CEASE NOT . . . MAKING MENTION OF YOU IN MY PRAYERS, that God . . . may give unto you the spirit of wisdom and revelation in the knowledge of him . . . that ye may know . . . what is the exceeding greatness of his power to us-ward who believe" (Eph. 1:16-19).

"FOR THIS CAUSE I BOW MY KNEES UNTO THE FATHER . . . that he would grant you . . . to be strengthened with might by his Spirit in the inner man; that Christ may dwell in your hearts by faith; that ye, being rooted . . . in love . . . might be filled with all the fullness of God" (Eph. 3:14-19).

"ALWAYS IN EVERY PRAYER OF MINE FOR YOU ALL, MAKING REQUEST with joy . . . I pray that your love may abound yet more and more . . . that ye may be sincere . . . filled with the fruits of righteousness" (Phil. 1:4-11).

"But my God shall supply all your need according to his riches in glory by Christ Jesus" (Phil. 4:19).

"WE . . . DO NOT CEASE TO PRAY FOR YOU, and to desire that ye might be filled with the knowledge of his will . . . that ye might walk worthy of the Lord . . . strengthened with all might according to his glorious power" (Col. 1:9-11). "I would that ye knew WHAT GREAT CONFLICT I HAVE FOR YOU . . . as many as have not seen my face in the flesh, that their hearts might be comforted, being knit together in love" (Col. 2:1-2).

What a study for the inner chamber! These passages teach us that unceasing prayer formed a large part of Paul's service in the gospel; we see the high spiritual aim which he set before himself, in his work on behalf of believers; and the tender and self-sacrificing love with which he ever continued to think of the Church and its needs. Let us ask God to bring each one of us, and all the ministers of His Word, to a life of which such prayer is the healthy and natural outflow. We shall need to turn again and again to these pages if we would really be brought by the Spirit to the apostolic life which God has given us as an example.

2. PAUL WAS A MINISTER WHO ASKED HIS CONGREGATION TO PRAY MUCH.—Read again with prayerful attention:

"I beseech you, brethren, for the Lord Jesus Christ's sake, and for the love of the Spirit, THAT YE STRIVE TOGETHER WITH ME IN YOUR PRAYERS TO GOD FOR ME; that I may be delivered from them that do not believe in Judea" (Rom. 15:30, 31).

"We . . . trust . . . in God . . . that he will yet deliver us, YE ALSO HELPING TOGETHER BY PRAYER FOR US" (II Cor. 1:9-11).

"PRAYING ALWAYS, WITH ALL PRAYER AND SUP-
PLICATION in the Spirit, and watching thereunto
with all perseverance and supplication for all
saints; AND FOR ME, that utterance may be given
unto me, that I may open my mouth boldly to
make known the mystery of the gospel . . . as I
ought to speak" (Eph. 6:18-20).

"For I know that this shall turn to my salvation, THROUGH YOUR PRAYER, and the supply of
the Spirit of Jesus Christ" (Phil. 1:19).

"CONTINUE IN PRAYER, and watch in the same
with thanksgiving, WITHAL PRAYING ALSO FOR US,
that God would open unto us a door of utterance,
to speak . . . as I ought to speak" (Col. 4:2-4).

"Finally, brethren, PRAY FOR US, that the word
of the Lord may have free course and be glorified,
even as it is with you" (II Thess. 3:1).

What a deep insight Paul had as to the unity of
the Body of Christ and the relation of the members one to another! It is as we permit the Holy
Spirit to work powerfully in us that He will reveal
this truth to us, and we too shall have this insight.
What a glimpse he gives us of the power of the
spiritual life among these Christians, by the way
in which he reckoned that at Rome, and Corinth,
and Ephesus, and Colosse, and Philippi, there were
men and women on whom he could rely for prayer
that would reach heaven and have power with God!
And what a lesson for all ministers, to lead them

to inquire if they truly appreciate the unity of the Body at its right value; if they are endeavoring to train up Christians as intercessors; and if they indeed understand that Paul had that confidence because he was himself so strong in prayer for the congregation! Let us learn the lesson and beseech God that ministers and congregations together may grow in the grace of prayer, so that their entire service and Christian life may witness that the Spirit of prayer rules them. Then we may be confident that God will avenge His own elect which cry out day and night unto Him.

Ministers of the Spirit

What is the meaning of the expression: "The minister of the gospel is a minister of the Spirit" (II Cor. 3:6-8)? It means:

1. *That the preacher is entirely under the power and control of the Spirit,* so that he may be led and used by the Spirit as He wills.

2. Many pray for the Spirit, that they may make use of Him and His power for their work. This is certainly wrong. It is He who must use you. Your relationship toward Him must be one of deep dependence and utter submission. *The Spirit must have you entirely, and always, and in all things under His power.*

3. There are many who think they must preach the Word only, and that the Spirit will make the Word fruitful. They do not understand that *it is the Spirit in and through the preacher who will bring the Word to the heart.* I must not be satisfied with praying to God to bless, through the operation of His Spirit, the Word that I preach. The Lord wants me to be filled with the Spirit: then I shall speak aright and my preaching will be in the manifestation of the Spirit and power.

4. We see this on the day of Pentecost. They were filled with the Spirit and began to speak, and spoke with power through the Spirit who was in them.

5. Thus we learn what the relationship of the minister toward the Spirit should be. He must have a strong belief that the Spirit is in him, that the Spirit will teach him in his daily life and will strengthen him to bear witness to the Lord Jesus in his preaching and visiting; he must live in ceaseless prayer that he may be kept and strengthened by the power of the Spirit.

6. When the Lord promised the apostles that they should receive power when the Holy Spirit had come upon them and commanded them to wait for Him, it was as though He had said: "Do not dare to preach without this power. It is the indispensable preparation for your work. Everything depends on it."

7. What then is the lesson we may learn from the phrase "ministers of the Spirit"? Alas, how little we have understood this! How little have we lived in it! How little have we experienced of the power of the Holy Spirit! What must we do then? There must be deep confession of guilt, that we have so constantly grieved the Spirit, because we have not lived daily as His ministers; and simple childlike surrender to His leading in sure confidence that the Lord will work a change in us; and further, daily fellowship with the Lord Jesus in ceaseless prayer. He will bestow on us the Holy Spirit as rivers of living water.

11

THE WORD AND PRAYER; PREACHING AND PRAYER; WHOLEHEARTEDNESS

LITTLE OF THE WORD with little prayer is death to the spiritual life. Much of the Word with little prayer gives a sickly life. Much prayer with little of the Word gives more life, but without steadfastness. A full measure of the Word and prayer each day gives a healthy and powerful life. Think of the Lord Jesus. In His youth and manhood He treasured the Word in His heart. In the temptation in the wilderness, and on every opportunity that presented itself—till He cried out on the cross in death, "My God, my God, why hast thou forsaken me?" He showed that the Word of God filled His heart. And in His prayer life He manifested two things: first, that the Word supplies us with material for prayer and encourages us in expecting everything from God. The second is that it is only by prayer that we can live such a life that every word of God can be fulfilled in us. And how then can we come to this, so that the Word and prayer may each have its undivided right over us? There is only one answer. Our lives must be wholly transformed. We must get a new, a healthy, a heavenly life, in which the hunger after God's Word and the thirst after God express themselves in prayer as naturally as do the needs of our earthly life. Every manifestation of the power of the flesh in us and the weakness of our spiritual life must drive us to the conviction that God will, through the powerful operation of His Holy Spirit, work out a new and strong life in us.

Oh, that we but understood that the Holy Spirit is essentially the Spirit of the Word and the Spirit of prayer! He will cause the Word to become a joy and a light in our souls, and He will also most surely help us in prayer to know the mind and will of God, and find in it our delight. If we as ministers wish to explain these things and to train God's people for the inheritance which is prepared for them, then we must commit ourselves from this moment forward to the leading of the Holy Spirit; must, in faith in what He will do in us, appropriate the heavenly life of Christ as He lived it here on earth, with certain expectation that the Spirit, who filled Him with the Word and prayer, will also accomplish that work in us.

Yes, let us believe that the Spirit who is in us is the Spirit of the Lord Jesus, and that He is in us to make us truly partakers of His life. If we firmly believe this and set our hearts upon it, then there will come a change in our intercourse with the Word and prayer such as we could not have thought possible. Believe it firmly; expect it surely.

We are familiar with the vision of the valley of dry bones. We know that the Lord said to the prophet: "Prophesy upon these bones . . . Behold, I will cause breath to enter into you, and ye shall live" (Ezek. 37:4, 5). And we know how, when he had done this, there was a noise, and bone came together to its bone, and flesh came up, and skin covered them—but there was no breath in them. The prophesying to the bones—the preaching of the Word of God—had a powerful influence. It was the beginning of the great miracle which was about to happen, and there lay an entire army of men newly made. It was the beginning of the work of life in them, but there was no spirit there.

How then the Lord said to the prophet: "Prophesy unto the wind . . . Thus saith the Lord God; Come from the four winds, O breath, and breathe upon these slain, that they may live" (verse 9). And when the prophet had done this, the Spirit came upon them, and they lived, and stood on their feet, a very great army. Prophesying to the bones, that is, *preaching*, has accomplished a great work. There lay the beautiful new bodies. But the prophesying to the Spirit, "Come, O Spirit," that is, *prayer,* accomplished a far more wonderful thing. The power of the Spirit was revealed through prayer.

Is not the work of our ministers mostly this prophesying to dry bones in making known the promises of God? This is followed sometimes by great results. Everything which belongs to the form of godliness has been brought to perfection; a careless congregation becomes regular and devout, but it remains true for the most part: "There is no life in them." Preaching must be followed by prayer. The preacher must come to see that his preaching is comparatively powerless to bring in a new life till he begins to take time for prayer and, according to the teaching of God's Word, strives and labors and continues in prayer, and takes no rest, and gives God no rest, till He bestows the Spirit in over-flowing power.

Do you not feel that a change must come in our work? We must learn from Peter to continue in prayer, in our ministry of the Word. Just as we are zealous preachers, we must be zealous in prayer. We must, with all our power, constantly like Paul, pray unceasingly. For the prayer: "Come, breathe on these slain," the answer is sure.

WHOLEHEARTEDNESS

Experience teaches us that if anyone is engaged in a work in which he is not wholehearted, he will seldom succeed. Just think of a student, or his teacher, a man of business, or a warrior. He who does not give himself wholeheartedly to his calling is not likely to succeed. And that is still more true of religion, and above all of the high and holy task of intercourse in prayer with a holy God and of being always well pleasing to Him. It is because of this that God has said so impressively: "Ye shall seek me and find me, WHEN YE SHALL SEARCH FOR ME WITH ALL YOUR HEART" (Jer. 29:13).

As also more than one of God's servants has said: "I seek Thee with my whole heart." Have you ever thought how many Christians there are of whom it is all too plain that they do not seek God with the whole heart? When they were in trouble over their sins, they seemed to seek God with the whole heart. But when they knew that they had been pardoned—one could see by their lives that they were religious, it is true—but no one would think: "This man has surrendered himself with his whole heart to follow God, and to serve Him as the supreme work of his life."

How is it with you? What does your heart say? While you, as minister for instance, have given yourself up with wholehearted devotion to fulfill your office faithfully and zealously, will you not perhaps acknowledge: "I fear, or rather I am convinced, that my unsatisfactory prayer life is to be attributed to nothing else than that I have not lived with a wholehearted surrender of all on earth that could hinder me in fellowship with God." What a deeply important question to consider in the inner chamber and to give the answer to God! How important to arrive at a plain answer and to utter it all before God! Prayerlessness cannot be overcome as an isolated thing. It is in the closest relationship to the state of the heart. True prayer depends on an undivided heart.

But I cannot give myself that undivided heart which can enable me to say: "I seek God WITH MY WHOLE HEART." No, that is impossible for you, but God will do it. "I will give them a heart to fear me." "I will write my law [as a power of life] in their heart." Such promises serve to awaken desire. However weak the desire may be, if there is but the sincere determination to strive after what God holds out to us, then He will Himself work in our hearts both to will and to do. It is the great work of the Holy Spirit in us to make us willing and to enable us to seek God with the whole heart. May there but be found in us confusion of face because, while we have given ourselves to so many earthly things with all our heart and strength, yet if anything is said about fellowship with our glorious God it so little affects us that we have not sought Him with the whole heart.

12

"FOLLOW ME"; THE HOLY TRINITY; LIFE AND PRAYER; PERSEVERANCE IN PRAYER; CARNAL OR SPIRITUAL

THE LORD did not speak these words to all who believed on Him, or who hoped to be blessed by Him, but to those whom He would make fishers of men. He said this not only at the first calling of the apostles, but also later on to Peter: "Henceforth thou shalt catch men." The holy art of winning souls, of loving and saving them, can be learned only in close and persistent intercourse with Christ. What a lesson for ministers and for Christian workers and others! This intercourse was the great and peculiar privilege of His disciples. The Lord chose them that they might be always with and near Him. We read of the choice of the twelve apostles in Mark 3:14: "And he ordained twelve that they might be *with him,* and that he might send them forth to preach." So also our Lord said on the last night (John 15:27): "And ye also shall bear witness, because ye have been *with me* from the beginning."

This fact was noticed by outsiders. Thus, for instance, the woman who spoke to Peter: "This man was also *with him*." So in the Sanhedrin: "They took knowledge of them, that they had been *with Jesus*." The chief characteristic and indispensable qualification for the man who will bear witness to Christ is that he has been with Him. Continuous fellowship with Christ is the only school for the training of ministers of the Holy Spirit. What a lesson for all ministers! It is only he who, like Caleb, follows the Lord fully, who will have power to teach other souls the art of following Jesus. But what an unspeakable grace that the Lord Jesus Himself would train us after His own likeness, so that others may learn from us! Then we might say with Paul to our converts: "Ye became followers of us and of the Lord." "Be ye followers of me, even as I also am of Christ."

Never was there a teacher who took such trouble with his scholars as Jesus Christ will with us who preach His Word. He will spare no pains; no time will be too precious or too long for Him. In the love which brought Him to the cross, He would hold intercourse, converse with us, fashion us, sanctify us, and make us fit for His holy service. Dare we still complain that it is too much for us to spend so much time in prayer? Shall we not

114

commit ourselves entirely to the love which gave up all for us, and look upon it as our greatest happiness now to hold fellowship with Him daily? Oh, all ye who long for blessing in your ministry, He calls you to be with Him. Let this be the greatest joy of your life; it will be the surest preparation for blessing in your service. O my Lord, draw me, help me, hold me fast, and teach me how daily to live in Thy fellowship by faith.

THE HOLY TRINITY

1. God is an ever flowing fountain of pure love and blessedness.

2. Christ is the reservoir wherein the fullness of God was made visible as grace, and has been opened for us.

3. The Holy Spirit is the stream of living water that flows from under the throne of God and of the Lamb.

4. The redeemed, God's believing children, are the channels through which the love of the Father, the grace of Christ, and the powerful operation of the Spirit are brought to the earth, there to be imparted to others.

5. What an impression we gain here of the wonderful partnership into which God takes us up, as dispensers of the grace of God! Prayer, when we chiefly pray for ourselves, is but the beginning of the

life of prayer. The glory of prayer is that we have power as intercessors to bring the grace of Christ, and the energizing power of the Spirit, upon those souls which are still in darkness.

6. The more surely the channel is connected with the reservoir, the more certainly will the water flow unhindered through it. The more we are occupied in prayer with the fullness of Christ, and with the Spirit who proceeds from Him, and the more firmly we abide in fellowship with Him, the more surely will our lives be happy and strong. This, however, is still only a preparation for the reality. The more we give ourselves up to fellowship and converse with the Triune God, the sooner shall we receive the courage and ability to pray down blessing on souls, on ministers, and on the Church around us.

7. Are you truly a channel which is always open, so that the water may flow through you to the thirsty ones in the dry land? Have you offered yourself unreservedly to God, to become a bearer of the energizing operations of the Holy Spirit?

8. Is it not, perhaps, because you have thought only of yourself in prayer that you have experienced so little of the power of prayer? Do understand that the new prayer life into which you have entered in the Lord Jesus can be sustained and strengthened only by the intercession in which you labor for the souls around you, to bring them to

know the Lord? Oh, meditate on this—God an ever flowing fountain of love and blessing, and I His child, a living channel through which every day the Spirit and life can be brought to the earth!

LIFE AND PRAYER

Our life has a great influence on our prayer; just as in the same way our prayer influences our life. The entire life of man is a continuous prayer, to nature or to the world, to provide for his wants and make him happy. This natural prayer and desire can be as strong in a man who also prays to God that the words of prayer which his mouth utters cannot be heard. God cannot at times hear the prayer of your lips because the desires of your heart after the world cry out to Him much more strongly and loudly.

The life exercises a mighty influence over prayer. A worldly life, a self-seeking life, makes prayer powerless and an answer impossible. With many Christians there is a conflict between the life and prayer, and the life holds the upper hand. *But prayer can also exercise a mighty influence over the life.* If I give myself entirely to God in prayer, then prayer can conquer the life of the flesh and sin. The entire life may be brought under the control of prayer. Prayer can change and renew the whole life, because prayer calls in and receives the

Lord Jesus and the Holy Spirit to purify and sanctify the life.

Many think that they must, with their defective spiritual life, work themselves up to pray more. They do not understand that only in proportion as the spiritual life is strengthened can the prayer life increase. Prayer and life are inseparably connected. What do you think? Which has the stronger influence over you, prayer for five or ten minutes, or the whole day spent in the desires of the world? Let it not surprise you if your prayers are not answered. The reason may easily lie here; your life and your prayer are at strife with each other; your heart is more wholly devoted to living than to prayer. Learn this great lesson: my prayer must rule my whole life. What I request from God in prayer is not decided in five or ten minutes. I must learn to say: "I have prayed with my whole heart." What I desire from God must really fill my heart the whole day; then the way is open for a certain answer.

Oh, the sacredness and power of prayer, if it takes possession of the heart and life! It keeps one constantly in fellowship with God. We can then literally say, "I wait on Thee all the day." Let us be careful to consider not only the length of the time we spend with God in prayer, but the power with which our prayer takes possession of our whole life.

"It is not reason," said Peter, "that we should leave the word of God, and serve tables" (Acts 6:2). For that work deacons were chosen. And this word of Peter serves for all time and for all who are set apart as ministers. "We will give ourselves continually to prayer, and to the ministry of the Word." Dr. Alexander Whyte, in an address, once said: "I think sometimes, when my salary is paid to me so faithfully and punctually: the deacons have performed faithfully their part of the agreement; have I been so faithful in my part, in persevering in prayer and the ministry of the Word?" Another minister has said: "How surprised people would be if I proposed to divide my time between these two equally—one-half given to prayer, the other to the ministry of the Word!"

Notice, in the case of Peter, what perseverance in prayer meant. He went up on the roof to pray. There, in prayer, he received heavenly instruction as to his work among the heathen. There, the message from Cornelius came to him. There, the Holy Spirit said to him: "Rise, and go with the three men who seek thee." And from there he went to Caesarea, where the Spirit was so unexpectedly outpoured on the heathen. All this is to teach us that it is through prayer God will give the instruction of His Spirit to make us understand His will, to let us know with whom we are to speak, to give us the assurance that His Spirit will make His Word powerful through us.

Have you ever earnestly thought over why it is that you have a salary and a parsonage, and are set free from the need of following earthly business? It is for nothing else than that you should continue in prayer and the ministry of the Word. That will be your wisdom and power. That will be the secret of a blessed service of the gospel.

No wonder that there is complaint about the ineffective spiritual life in minister and congregation, while that which is of prime importance, perseverance in prayer, does not hold its rightful place—the first place.

Peter was able to speak and act as he did because he was filled with the Spirit. Let us not be satisfied with anything less than hearty surrender to an undivided appropriation of the Spirit, as Leader and Lord of our lives. Nothing less will help us. Then, for the first time, we shall be able to say: "God hath made us able ministers of his Spirit."

CARNAL OR SPIRITUAL?

There is a great difference between those two states which is but little understood or pondered. The Christian who walks in the Spirit and has crucified the flesh, is spiritual (Gal. 5:24). The Christian who walks after the flesh and wishes to please the flesh is carnal (Rom. 13:14). The Galatians, who had begun in the Spirit were ending in the flesh. Yet there were among them some spiritual members who were able to restore the wandering with meekness.

What a difference between the carnal and the spiritual Christian (I Cor. 3:1-3)! With the carnal Christian there may be much religion and much zeal for God, and for the service of God. But it is for the most part in human power. With the spiritual, on the other hand, there is a complete subjection to the leading of the Spirit, a deep sense of weakness and entire dependence on the work of Christ—it is a life of abiding fellowship with Christ, wrought out by the Spirit.

How important for me it is to find out and plainly to acknowledge before God whether I am spiritual or carnal! A minister may be very faithful in his orthodoxy, and be most zealous in his service, and yet be so, chiefly, in the power of human wisdom and zeal. And one of the signs of this is that there is little pleasure or perseverance in fellowship with Christ through prayer. Love of prayer is one of the marks of the Spirit.

What a change is necessary for a Christian who is chiefly carnal to become truly spiritual! At first he cannot understand what must happen, or how it can come to pass. The more the truth dawns upon him, the more he is convinced that it is impossible, *unless God does it*. Yet to believe truly that God will do it requires earnest prayer. Quiet retirement and meditation are indispensable, along with the death of all confidence in ourselves. But along this road there ever comes the faith that *God can, God is willing, God will do it.* The soul which earnestly clings to the Lord Jesus will be led by the Spirit to this faith.

How will you be able to say to others :"I cannot speak unto you as unto spiritual, but as unto carnal, even as unto babes in Christ"? (I Cor. 3:1). It is impossible unless you yourself have the experience of having passed from the one state to the other. But God will teach you. Persevere in prayer and faith.

13

GEORGE MUELLER; HUDSON TAYLOR; LIGHT FROM THE INNER CHAMBER

JUST AS GOD gave the apostle Paul as an example in his prayer life for Christians of all time, so He has also given George Mueller in these latter days as a proof to His Church how literally and wonderfully He still always hears prayer. It is not only that He gave him in his lifetime over a million pounds sterling to support his orphanages, but Mr. Mueller also stated that he believed that the Lord had given him more than thirty thousand souls in answer to prayer. And that not only from among the orphans, but also many others for whom he (in some cases for fifty years) had prayed faithfully every day, in the firm faith that they would be saved. When he was asked on what ground he so firmly believed this, his answer was: "There are five conditions which I always endeavor to fulfill, in observing which I have the assurance of answer to my prayer:

1. "I have not the least doubt because I am assured that it is the Lord's will to save them, for He willeth that all men should be saved and come to the knowledge of the truth (I Tim. 2:4); and we have the assurance 'that if we ask anything according to his will, he heareth us' (I John 5:14).

2. "I have never pleaded for their salvation in my own name, but in the blessed name of my precious Lord Jesus, and on His merits alone (John 1:14).

3. "I always firmly believed in the willingness of God to hear my prayers (Mark 11:24).

4. "I am not conscious of having yielded to any sin, for 'if I regard iniquity in my heart, the Lord will not hear me' when I call (Ps. 66:18).

5. "I have persevered in believing prayer for more than fifty-two years for some, and shall continue till the answer comes: 'Shall not God avenge his own elect which cry day and night unto him?'" (Luke 18:7).

Take these thoughts into your hearts and practice prayer according to these rules. Let prayer be not only the utterance of your desires, but a fellowship with God, till we know by faith that our prayer is heard. The way George Mueller walked is the new and living way to the throne of grace, which is open for us all.

HUDSON TAYLOR

When Hudson Taylor, as a young man, had given himself over unreservedly to the Lord, there came to him a strong conviction that God would send him to China. He had read of George Mueller and how God had answered his prayers for his own support and that of his orphans, and he began to ask the Lord to teach him also so to trust Him. He felt that if he would go to China with such faith, he must first begin to live by faith in England. He asked the Lord to enable him to do this. He had a position as a doctor's dispenser, and asked God to help him not to ask for his salary, but to leave it to God to move the heart of the doctor to pay him at the right time. The doctor was a good-hearted man, but very irregular in payment. This cost Taylor much trouble and struggle in prayer because he believed, as did George Mueller, that the word, "Owe no man anything," was to be taken literally, and that debt should not be incurred.

So he learned the great lesson *to move men through God*—a thought of deep meaning, which later on became an unspeakably great blessing to him in his work in China. He relied on that—in the conversion of the Chinese, in the awakening of Christians to give money for the support of the work, in the finding of suitable missionaries who would hold as faith's rule of conduct that we should make *our desires known to God in prayer and then rely on God to move men to do what He would have done.*

After he had been for some years in China, he prayed that God would give twenty-four missionaries, two for each of the eleven provinces and Mongolia, each with millions of souls and with no missionary. God did it. But there was no society to send them out. He had indeed learned to trust God for his own support, but he dared not take upon himself the responsibility of the twenty-four, if possibly they had not sufficient faith. This cost him severe conflict, and he became very ill under it, till at last he saw that God could as easily care for the twenty-four as for himself. He undertook it in a glad faith. And so God led him, through many severe trials of faith, to trust Him fully. Now these twenty-four have increased, in course of time, to a thousand missionaries who rely wholly on God for support. Other missionary societies have acknowledged how much they have learned from Hudson Taylor, as a man who stated and obeyed this law. *Faith may rely on God to move men to do what His children have asked of Him in prayer.*

Read the book.[1] There will be found in it a treasure of spiritual thought and experience con-

---

[1] *Hudson Taylor's Early Years*, by Dr. and Mrs. Howard Taylor, China Inland Mission.

cerning a close walk with God in the inner chamber and in mission work.

LIGHT FROM THE INNER CHAMBER

"But thou, when thou prayest, enter into thy closet, and when thou hast shut thy door, pray to thy Father which is in secret; and thy Father which seeth in secret shall reward thee openly."—Matthew 6:6

Our Lord had spoken of the prayer of the hypocrites who desire to be seen of men and also of the prayer of the heathen who trust in the multitude of their words. They do not understand that prayer has no value except it is addressed to a personal God who sees and hears. In the text our Lord teaches us a wonderful lesson concerning the inestimable blessing which the Christian may have in his inner chamber. If we would understand the lesson aright, we must notice the light that the inner chamber sheds on.

1. THE WONDERFUL LOVE OF GOD. Think of God, His greatness, His holiness, His unspeakable glory, and then on the inestimable privilege to which He invites His children, that each one of them, however sinful or feeble he may be, every hour of the day, may have access to Him and hold converse with Him as long as he wishes. If he enters his inner chamber, then God is ready *to meet him, to have fellowship with him, to give him*

the joy and strength which he needs with the living assurance in his heart that He is with him and will undertake for him in everything. In addition He promises that He will enrich him in his outward life and work with those things which he has asked for in secret. Ought we not to cry out with joy? What an honor! What a salvation! What an overflowing supply for every need!

One may be in the greatest distress, or may have fallen into the deepest sin, or may in the ordinary course of life desire temporal or spiritual blessing; he may desire to pray for himself or for those belonging to him, or for his congregation or church; he may even become an intercessor for the whole world—the promise for the inner chamber covers all: "Pray to thy Father which is in secret; he will reward thee openly."

We might well suppose that there would be no place on earth so attractive to the child of God as the inner chamber with the presence of God promised, where he may have unhindered intercourse with the Father. The happiness of a child on earth if he enjoys the love of his father; the happiness of a friend as he meets a beloved benefactor; the happiness of a subject who has free access to his king and may stay with him as long as he wishes; these are as nothing compared with this heavenly promise. In the inner chamber you can converse with your God as long and as intimately as you desire; you can rely on His presence and fellowship.

Oh, the wonderful love of God in the gift of an inner chamber sanctified by such a promise! *Let us thank God every day of our lives for it* as the gift of His wonderful love. In this sinful world He could devise nothing more suitable for our needs than a fountain of unspeakable blessing.

2. THE DEEP SINFULNESS OF MAN. We might have thought that every child of God would have availed himself with joy of such an invitation. But, see! what is the response? There comes a cry from all lands that prayer in the inner chamber is, as a general rule, neglected by those who call themselves believers. Many make no use of it; they go to church, they confess Christ, but they know little of personal intercourse with God. Many make a little use of it, but in a spirit of haste, and more as a matter of custom, or for the easing of conscience, so that they cannot speak of any joy or blessing in it. And, what is more sad, many who know something of its blessedness confess that they know little about faithful, regular, and happy fellowship with the Father, all the day, as something which is as necessary as their daily bread.

Oh, what is it, then, that makes the inner chamber so powerless? Is it not the deep sinfulness of man, and the aversion of his fallen nature for God, *which make the world with its fellowship more attractive than being alone with the heavenly Father?*

Is it not that Christians do not believe the Word of God, where that Word declares that "the flesh" which is in them, "is enmity against God," and that they walk too much after "the flesh," so that the Spirit cannot strengthen them for prayer? Is it not that Christians allow themselves to be deprived by Satan of the use of the weapon of prayer, so that they are powerless to overcome him? Oh, the deep sinfulness of man! *We have no greater proof of it than this despite that is done to the unspeakable love which has given us the inner chamber.*

And what is still more sad is that even ministers of Christ acknowledge that they know they pray too little. The Word tells them that their only power lies in prayer: through that only, and through that certainly, they can be clothed with power from on high for their work. But it seems as though the power of the world and the flesh has bewitched them. While they devote time to and manifest zeal in their work, that which is the most necessary of all is neglected, and there is not the desire or strength for prayer to obtain the indispensable gift of the Holy Spirit to make their work fruitful. God give us grace to understand in the light of the inner chamber the deep sinfulness of our nature.

3. THE GLORIOUS GRACE OF CHRIST JESUS. Is there, then, no hope of a change? Must it be al-

ways thus? Or is there a means of recovery? Thank God! there is.

The man through whom God has made known to us the message of the inner chamber is no other than our Lord Jesus Christ, who saves us from our sins. He is able and willing to deliver us from this sin, and will deliver. He has not undertaken to redeem us from all our other sins and left us to deal with the sin of prayerlessness in our own strength. No, in this also we may come to Him and cry out, "Lord, if thou wilt thou canst make me clean." "Lord, I believe, help thou mine unbelief."

Do you wish to know how you may experience this deliverance? By none other than the well-known way along which every sinner must come to Christ. Begin by acknowledging, by confessing before Him, in a childlike and simple manner, the sin of neglecting and desecrating the inner chamber. Bow before Him in deep shame and sorrow. Tell Him that your heart has deceived you by the thought that you could pray as you ought. Tell Him that through the weakness of "the flesh," and the power of the world, and self-confidence, you have been led astray and that you have no strength to do better. Let this be done heartily. You cannot by your resolution and effort put things right.

Come in your sin and weakness to the inner chamber, and *begin to thank God, as you have never thanked Him,* that the grace of the Lord Jesus will surely make it possible for you to converse with your Father as a child ought to do. Hand over afresh to the Lord Jesus all your sin and misery, as well as your whole life and will, that He may cleanse and take possession of you and rule over you as His very own.

Even though your heart be cold and dead, persevere in the exercise of faith that Christ is an almighty and faithful Saviour. You may be sure that deliverance will come. Expect it, and you will begin to understand that the inner chamber is the revelation of the glorious grace of the Lord Jesus, which makes it possible for one to do what he could not do himself; that is, to hold fellowship with God, and to experience that the desire and power are received which fit a man for walking with God.

14

THE CROSS SPIRIT IN OUR LORD

WE SEEK SOMETIMES for the operation of the
Spirit, with the object of obtaining more power for
work, more love in the life, more holiness in the
heart, more light on Scripture or on our path. And
yet all these gifts are only subordinate to what is
the great purpose of God. The Father has bestowed
the Spirit on the Son, and the Son has given Him
to us, with the one great object of revealing and
glorifying Christ Jesus Himself in us.

The heavenly Christ must become for us a real
living personality, always with us and in us. Our
life on earth must be every day lived in the unbroken and holy fellowship of our Lord Jesus in
heaven. This must be the first and the greatest work
of the Holy Spirit in believers, that they should
know and experience Christ as the life of their life.
God desires that we should become strengthened
with might by His Spirit in the inner man, that
Christ may dwell in our hearts through faith, and

that so we may be filled with His love unto all the fullness of God.

This was the secret of the joy of the first disciples. They had received the Lord Jesus, whom they feared they had lost, as the heavenly Christ into their hearts.

And this was their preparation for Pentecost: *they were entirely taken up with Him.* He was literally their all. Their hearts were empty of everything, so that the Spirit might fill them with Christ. In the fullness of the Spirit they had power for a life and service such as the Lord desired. Is this, now, with us, the great object in our desires, in our prayers, in our experience? The Lord teach us to know that the blessing for which we have so earnestly prayed can be preserved and increased in no other way than through *intimate fellowship with Christ in the inner chamber,* every day practiced and cultivated.

And yet it has seemed to me that there was a still deeper secret of Pentecost to be discovered. The thought came that perhaps our conception of the Lord Jesus in heaven was limited. We think of Him in the splendor, the glory of God's throne. We also think of the unsearchable love which moved Him to give Himself for us. But we forget too often that, above all, it is as the crucified One He was known here on earth; and that, above all, it is as the crucified One He has His place on the

throne of God. "And lo, in the midst of the throne
. . . stood a Lamb as it has been slain" (Rev. 5:6).

Yes, it is as the crucified One that He is the
object of the Father's eternal good pleasure and
of the worship of the entire creation. And it is,
therefore, of the first importance, that we here on
earth should know and have experience of Him as
the crucified One, so that we may make men see
what His disposition and ours is, and what the
power is that can make them partakers of salvation.

I feel deeply that, as the cross is Christ's highest
glory, and as the Holy Spirit neither has done nor
can do anything greater or more glorious than He
did when "he through the eternal Spirit offered himself without spot to God"; so it is evident that the
Holy Spirit can do nothing greater or more glorious
for us than to take us up into the fellowship of that
cross, and to work out also in us the same spirit
of the cross which was seen in our Lord Jesus. In
a word, the question arose whether this was not the
real reason why our prayers for the powerful operation of the Holy Spirit could not be answered, because we had sought too little to receive the Spirit,
in order that *we might know and become like the
glorified Christ in the fellowship of His cross.*

Have we not here the deepest secret of Pente-
cost? The Spirit comes to us from the cross, where
He strengthened Christ to offer Himself to God.
He comes from the Father, who looked down with

unspeakable good pleasure of the humiliation and obedience and self-sacrifice of Christ, as the highest proof of His surrender to Him. He comes from Christ, who through the cross was prepared to receive from the Father the fullness of the Spirit, that He might share it with the world. He comes to reveal *Christ to our hearts, as the Lamb slain, in the midst of the throne,* so that we on earth may worship Him as they do in heaven. He comes, chiefly, to impart to us the life of the crucified Christ, so that we may be able to say truly, "I am crucified with Christ; I live, yet not I; Christ liveth in me."

To understand this secret in any way, we must first meditate on what the meaning and what the worth of the cross is.

THE MIND THAT WAS IN THE CRUCIFIED CHRIST

The cross must necessarily be viewed from two standpoints. First, the work it has accomplished— the pardon and conquest of sin. This is the first message with which the cross comes to the sinner. It proclaims to him free and full deliverance from the power of sin. And then the second, the spirit or disposition which was there manifested. We find this expressed in Philippians 2:8: "He humbled himself, and became obedient unto death, even the death of the cross." Here we see *self-abasement* to the lowest place which could be found under the burden of our sin and curse; *obedience* to the uttermost to all the will of God; *self-sacrifice* to the death of the cross—these three words reveal to us the holy perfection of His Person and work. Therefore God hath so greatly exalted Him. It was the spirit of the cross which made Him the object of His Father's good pleasure, of the worship of the angels, of the love and confidence of all the redeemed. The self-abasement of Christ, His obedience to the will of God even to death, His self-sacrifice even to the death of the cross—these made Him to be "the Lamb, as it had been slain, standing in the midst of the throne."

The Spirit of the Cross in Us

All that Christ was, He was for us and *desires to become in us*. The spirit of the cross was His blessedness and glory. It should be this even more for us. He desires to manifest His likeness in us and to give us a full share of all that is His. Thus Paul writes the words we have so often quoted: "Let this mind be in you, which was also in Christ Jesus." Elsewhere he writes: "We have the mind of Christ." The fellowship of the cross is not only a holy duty for us, but an unspeakably blessed privilege, which the Holy Spirit Himself will make ours according to the promise: "He shall take of mine,

and shall show it unto you"; "He shall glorify me."
The Holy Spirit wrought this disposition in Christ
and will also work it in us.

15

TAKING UP THE CROSS

When the Lord told His disciples that they must take up the cross and follow Him, they could have little understanding of His meaning. He wished to rouse them to earnest thought and so prepare them for the time when they should see Him carrying His cross. From the Jordan, where He had presented Himself to be baptized and reckoned among sinners, onward, He carried the cross always in His heart. That is to say, He was always conscious that the sentence of death, because of sin, rested on Him, and that He must bear it to the uttermost. As the disciples thought on this and wondered what He meant by it, one thing only helped them—it was the thought of a man who was sentenced to death, and carried his cross to the appointed place.

Christ had said at the same time: "He that loseth his life shall find it." He taught them that they must hate their own life. Their nature was so sinful that nothing less than death could meet their need; it deserved nothing less than death. So the conviction gradually dawned upon them that the taking up of the cross meant: "I am to feel that my life is under sentence of death, and that under the consciousness of this sentence I must constantly surrender my flesh, my sinful nature, to death." So they were slowly prepared to see later on that the cross which Christ had carried was the one power to deliver truly from sin, and that they must first receive from Him the true cross spirit. They must learn from Him what self-humiliation in their weakness and unworthiness was to mean; what the obedience was which crucified their own will in all things, in the greatest as well as in the least; what the self-denial was which did not seek to please the flesh or the world. "Take thy cross and follow me"—that was the word with which Jesus prepared His disciples for the great thought that His mind and disposition might become theirs, that His cross might in very deed become their own.

CRUCIFIED WITH CHRIST

The lesson which the Lord wished His disciples to learn from His statement concerning the taking up of the cross and the losing of their life finds its expression in the words of Paul, after Christ had died on the cross and had been exalted on high, and the Spirit had been poured out. Paul says: "I am crucified with Christ. . . . God forbid that I should glory, save in the cross of our Lord Jesus Christ, by whom the world is crucified unto me, and I unto the world" (Gal. 2:20; 6:14). He wished every believer to live so as to prove that he was crucified with Christ. He wished us to understand that the Christ who comes to dwell in our hearts is the crucified Christ, who will Himself, through His life, impart to us the true mind of the cross. He tells us that "our old man is crucified with Him." Yea, more, that "they who are Christ's have crucified the flesh." When they received by faith the crucified Christ, they gave over the flesh to the death sentence which was executed to the full on Calvary. Paul says "we have been planted together in the likeness of his death" (Rom. 6:5), and that therefore we must reckon that we are dead to sin in Christ Jesus.

These words of the Holy Spirit, through Paul, teach us that we must abide constantly in the fellowship of the cross, in fellowship with the crucified and living Lord Jesus. It is the soul that lives ever under the cover and shelter and deliverance of the cross that alone can expect constantly to glory in Christ Jesus and in His abiding nearness.

THE FELLOWSHIP OF THE CROSS

There are many who place their hope for salvation in the redemption of the cross who understand little about the fellowship of the cross. They rely

on what the cross has purchased for them, on forgiveness of sin and peace with God; but they can
often live for a length of time without fellowship
with the Lord Himself. They do not know what it
means to strive every day after heart communion
with the crucified Lord as He is seen in heaven—
"A Lamb in the midst of the throne." Oh, that this
vision might exercise its spiritual power upon us,
that we might really experience every day that as
truly as the Lamb is seen there on the throne, so
we may have the power and experience of His
presence here!

Is it possible? Without doubt it is. Why did
that great miracle happen, and why was the Holy
Spirit given from heaven, if it were not to make
the glorified Jesus—"the Lamb standing, as slain,
in the midst of the throne"—present with us here
in our earthly surroundings? Let us endeavor to
make this more plain in our further meditations.

16

THE HOLY SPIRIT
AND THE CROSS

THE HOLY SPIRIT ever leads us to the cross. It was so with Christ. The Spirit taught Him and enabled Him to offer Himself without spot to God.

It was so with the disciples. The Spirit, with whom they were filled, led them to preach Christ as the crucified One. Later on He led them to glory in the fellowship of the cross when they were deemed worthy to suffer for Christ's sake.

And the cross directed them again to the Spirit. When Christ had borne the cross, He received the Spirit from the Father, that He might be poured out. When the three thousand bowed before the crucified One, they received the promise of the Holy Spirit. When the disciples rejoiced in their experience of the fellowship of the cross, they received the Holy Spirit afresh. The union between the Spirit and the cross is indissoluble; they belong inseparably to one another. We see this especially in the epistles of Paul. "Jesus Christ hath been evidently set forth, crucified among you. . . . Received ye the Spirit by the works of the law, or by the hearing of faith?" (Gal. 3:1, 2).

"Christ hath redeemed us from the curse of the law . . . that we might receive the promise of the Spirit through faith" (Gal. 3:13, 14). "God sent his Son . . . to redeem them that were under the law . . . and . . . hath sent forth the Spirit of his Son into your hearts" (Gal. 4:4-6). "And they that are Christ's have crucified the flesh . . . If we live in the Spirit, let us also walk in the Spirit" (Gal. 5:24, 25). "Ye also are become dead to the law by the body of Christ . . . that we should serve in newness of spirit" (Rom. 7:4-6). "For the law of the Spirit of life in Christ Jesus hath made me free from the law of sin and death. For . . . God . . . condemned sin in the flesh, that the righteousness of the law might be fulfilled in us, who walk not after the flesh, but after the Spirit" (Rom. 8:2-4).

In everything and always the Spirit and the cross are inseparable. Yes, even in heaven. The Lamb, as it had been slain, standing in the midst of the throne had "seven eyes, *which are the seven Spirits of God* sent forth into all the earth" (Rev. 5:6). Again: "He showed me a pure river of water of life, clear as crystal [Is this other than the Holy Spirit?], proceeding out of the throne of God and

144

of the Lamb" (Rev. 22:1). When Moses smote the rock, the water streamed out and Israel drank. When the Rock Christ was actually smitten and He had taken His place as the slain Lamb on the throne of God, there flowed out from under the throne the fullness of the Holy Spirit for the whole world.

How foolish it is to pray for the fullness of the Spirit if we have not first placed ourselves under the full power of the cross! Just think of the one hundred and twenty disciples. The crucifixion of Christ had touched, broken, and taken possession of their entire hearts. They could speak or think of nothing else, and when the crucified One had shown them His hands and His feet, He said unto them: *"Receive ye the Holy Ghost."* And so also, with their hearts full of the crucified Christ, now received up into heaven, they were prepared to be filled with the Spirit. They dared to proclaim to the people: "Repent and believe in the crucified One"; and they also received the Holy Spirit.

Christ gave Himself up entirely to the cross. The disciples also did the same. The cross demands this also from us; it would have our entire life. To comply with this demand requires nothing less than a powerful act of the will, for which we are unfit, and a powerful act of God of which he may be assured who casts himself, in helplessness, but unreservedly on God.

THE SPIRIT AND THE CROSS

Why are there not more men and women who can witness, in the joy of their hearts, that the Spirit of God has taken possession of them and given them new power to witness for Him? Yet more urgently arises the heart-searching question to which an answer must be given: What is it that hinders? The Father in heaven is more willing than an earthly father to give bread to his child, and yet the cry arises: "Is the Spirit straitened? Is this His work?"

Many will acknowledge that the hindrance undoubtedly lies in the fact that the Church is too much under the sway of the flesh and the world. They understand too little of the heart-piercing power of the cross of Christ. So it comes to pass that the Spirit has not the vessels into which He can pour His fullness.

Many complain that the subject is too high or too deep for them. This is a proof of how little we have appropriated and brought into practice the teaching of Paul and Christ about the cross. I bring you a message of joy. The Spirit who is in you, in however limited a measure, is prepared to take you under His teaching, to lead you to the cross, and by His heavenly instruction to make you know something of what the crucified Christ wills to do for you and in you.

But then He wants you to take time, so that He may reveal the heavenly mysteries to you. He wants to make you see how the neglect of the inner chamber has hindered fellowship with Christ, the knowledge of the cross, and the powerful operations of the Spirit. He will teach you what is meant by the denial of self, the taking up of your cross, the losing of your life, and following Him.

In spite of all that you have felt of your ignorance, and lack of spiritual insight and fellowship with the cross, He is able and willing to take you under His teaching and to make known to you the secret of the spiritual life above all your expectations.

Begin at the beginning. Be faithful in the inner chamber. Thank Him that you can reckon on Him to meet you there. Although everything appears cold, and dark, and strained, bow in silence before the loving Lord Jesus, who so longs after you. Thank the Father that He has given you the Spirit. And be assured that all you do not yet know, and still must know—about "the flesh," and "the world," and the cross—the Spirit of Christ, who is in you, will surely make known to you. O soul, only believe that this blessing is for you! Christ belongs entirely to you. He longs to obtain full possession of you. He can and will possess you through the Holy Spirit. But for this, time is necessary. Oh, give Him time in the inner chamber every day. You can rest assured that He will fulfill His promise in you. "He that loveth me keepeth my commandments, and my Father will love him, and *I will manifest myself to him.*"

Persevere, in addition to all that you ask for yourself, in prayer for your congregation, your church, your minister; for all believers; for the whole Church of God, that God may strengthen them with power through His Spirit, so that Christ may dwell in their hearts by faith. Blessed time when the answer comes! Continue in prayer. The Spirit will reveal and glorify Christ and His love, Christ and His cross "as the Lamb slain standing in the midst of the throne."

THE CROSS AND THE FLESH

These two are deadly enemies. The cross desires to condemn and put to death "the flesh." "The flesh" desires to cast aside and conquer the cross. Many, as they hear of the cross as the indispensable preparation for the fullness of the Holy Spirit, will find out what there is in them which must yet be crucified. We must understand that our entire nature is sentenced to death and become dead by the cross, so that the new life in Christ may come to rule in us. We must obtain such an insight into the fallen condition of our nature and its enmity against God that we become willing, nay desirous, to be wholly freed from it.

We must learn to say with Paul: "In me, that is in my flesh, dwelleth no good thing." "The mind of the flesh is enmity against God: it is not subject to the law of God, neither indeed can be." It is its very essence to hate God and His holy law. This is the wonder of redemption, that Christ has borne on the cross the judgment and curse of God of "the flesh," and has forever nailed it to the cursed tree. If a man only believes God's Word about this "cursed mind of the flesh," and then longs to be delivered from it, he learns to love the cross as his deliverer from the power of the enemy.

"Our old man is crucified" with Christ, and our one hope is to receive this by faith and to hold it fast. "They that are Christ's have crucified the flesh." They have willingly declared that they will daily regard "the flesh" which is in them as the enemy of God, the enemy of Christ, the enemy of their soul's salvation, and will treat it as having received its deserved reward in being nailed to the cross.

This is one part of the eternal redemption which Christ has brought to us. It is not something which we can grasp with our understanding or accomplish with our strength. It is something which the Lord Jesus Himself will give us if we are willing to abide in His fellowship day by day, and to receive everything from Him. It is something which the Holy

Spirit will teach us, and He will impart it to us as an experience, and will show how He can give victory in the power of the cross over all that is of the flesh.

THE CROSS AND THE WORLD

What the flesh is in the smallest circle of my own person, that the world is in the larger circle of mankind. "The flesh" and "the world" are two manifestations of the same "god of this world" who is served by both. When the cross deals with "the flesh" as accursed, we at once discover what the nature and power of the world are. "They hated both me and my Father." The proof of this was that they crucified Christ. But Christ obtained the victory on the cross and freed us from the power of "the world." And now we can say: "God forbid that I should glory, save in the cross of our Lord Jesus Christ, by whom the world is crucified unto me, and I unto the world."

The cross was to Paul every day a holy reality, both in what he had to suffer from the world and in the victory which the cross constantly gave. John also writes: "The whole world lieth in wickedness" (I John 5:19). "Who is he that overcometh the world, but he that believeth that Jesus is the Son of God? This is he that came by water and blood, even Jesus Christ. . . . And it is the Spirit that beareth witness, because the Spirit is truth"

(I John 5:5, 6). Against the two great powers of the god of this world, God has given us two great powers from heaven, namely, the cross and the Spirit.

A TESTIMONY

IN THE FOLLOWING QUOTATIONS from *Starlight*,[1] by G. Sterrenberg, the great truth about the cross is expressed in simple and powerful words. Let the chapters on "The Fellowship of the Cross" and "The Holy Spirit and the Cross" especially be read.

Our Head Christ took the lowest place on the cross, and so He has marked out for us His members the lowest place. The brightness of God's glory (Heb. 1:3) became the rejected of men (Isaiah 53:4). Since that time the only right we have is to be the last and the lowest. When we claim anything more we have not yet rightly understood the cross.

We *seek for a higher life;* we shall find it if we sink deeper into the cross fellowship with our Lord. God has given the crucified One the highest place (Rev. 5). Shall we not do the same? We do this when from hour to hour we act as those who are crucified with Him (Gal. 2:19, 20). Thus we honor the crucified Lord.

---

[1]Now out of print

We *long for full victory*. We find this as we more fully enter into the fellowship of His cross. The Lamb obtained His greatest victory with His hands and feet nailed to the cross. We abide in the shadow of the Almighty only so long as we abide under the shadow of the cross. The cross must be our home. There alone are we sheltered. We first understand our own cross when we have understood His. And we desire to get so close to it that we not only view it but touch it, yes, still more that we take up the cross, and so it becomes as someone has said, an inner cross. Then the cross asserts itself in us, and we experience His power which especially manifests itself in this, that we do not faint under it but carry it with joy.

What would Jesus be without His cross? His pierced feet have bruised the head of the enemy, and His pierced hands have despoiled him utterly (Matt. 12:29). What are we without the cross? Do not let the cross go, but hold it fast. Do we think that we can go by another road than that He trod? Many can make no progress because they will not take up the cross.

EPILOGUE

A SINGLE WORD to the reader concerning the disposition of mind to which this book appeals! It is not enough that one should understand and appropriate the thought of the writer, and then rejoice because of the new insight he has obtained and the pleasure which knowledge has brought. There is something else which is of great importance. I must surrender myself to the truth so that I shall be ready, with an undivided will, immediately to perform all that I shall learn to be God's will.

In a book such as this, dealing with the life of prayer and hidden fellowship with God, it is indispensable that we should be prepared to receive and obey all that we see to be according to the Word and will of God. Where this disposition is lacking, knowledge only serves to make the heart less capable of receiving fuller life. Satan endeavors to become master of the Christian's inner chamber because he knows that if there has been unfaithfulness in prayer the testimony will bring but little loss to his kingdom. Spiritual power to lead the unsaved to the Lord, or to build up the children of

God, will not be experienced under it. Persevering prayer, through which alone this power comes, has been lacking.

The great living question has been before many: Shall we really set ourselves to win back again the weapon of believing prayer which Satan has, in a measure, taken away from us? Let us set before ourselves the serious importance of this conflict. As far as each minister is concerned, everything depends on whether or not he is a man of prayer—one who in the inner chamber must be clothed each day with power from on high. We, in common with the Church throughout the whole world, have to complain that prayer has not the place in our service of God that it ought to have, according to the will and promise of God and according to the need of minister and congregation and church.

The public consecration which many a believer has been led to make of himself at conferences is not an easy thing. And even when the step is taken, old custom, and the power of the flesh, will tend to bring it to naught. The power of faith is not yet vigorous. It will cost strife and sacrifice to conquer the devil in the name of Christ. Our churches are the battlefield where Satan will bring forth all his power to prevent us from becoming men of prayer, powerful in the Lord to obtain the victory in heaven and on earth. How much depends on this for ourselves, for our congregations, and for the kingdom!

Do not be surprised if I say that it is with fear and trembling, and not without much prayer, that I have written what I trust will help to encourage the brethren in the conflict. It is with a feeling of deep unworthiness that I venture to offer myself as a guide to the inner chamber, which is the way to holiness and to fellowship with God.

Do not wonder that I have asked the Lord that He would give this book a place in some inner chambers, and that He may assist the reader, so that, as he sees what God's will is, he may immediately give himself up to the doing of it. In war, everything depends on each soldier being obedient to the word of command, even though it costs him his life. In our strife with Satan we shall not conquer unless each one of us holds himself ready even in the reading of this simple book, to say from the heart: "What God says I will do; and if I see that anything is according to His will, I will immediately receive it and act upon it."

Do not wonder that I have written this testimony to remind the brethren that everything depends on the spirit of surrender to immediate obedience, in which we read all that is said according to the Word of God.

God grant that, in His great grace, this book may prove a bond of fellowship by which we may think of and help one another, and strengthen each other for the conflict in prayer by which the enemy may be overcome and the life of God may be gloriously revealed!